AF572162

peep • show

vicky wetherill

dewi lewis publishing

peep: *vb. (intr)* 1. to look furtively
or secretly, as through a small
aperture or from a hidden place.
2. to appear partially or briefly.
~ *n.* 3. a quick or furtive look.
4. the first appearance.

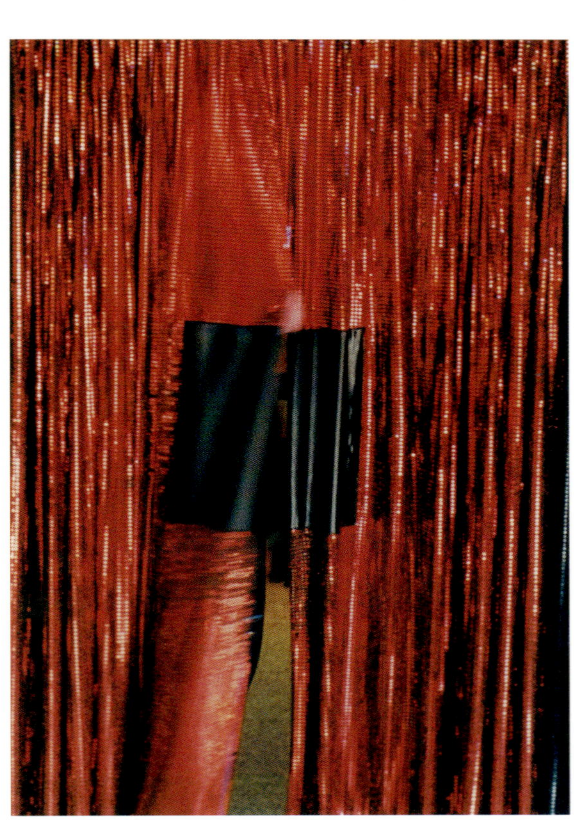

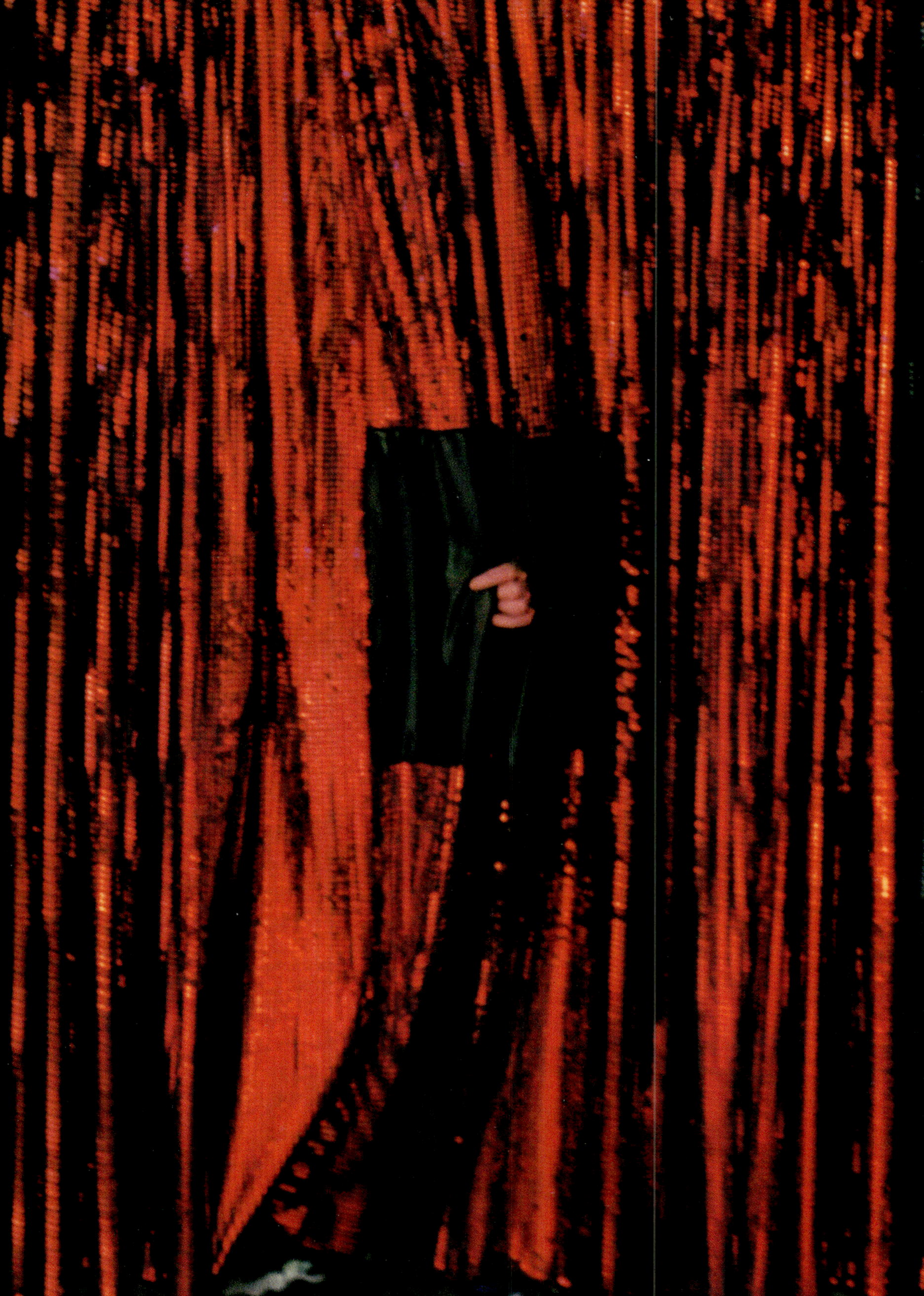

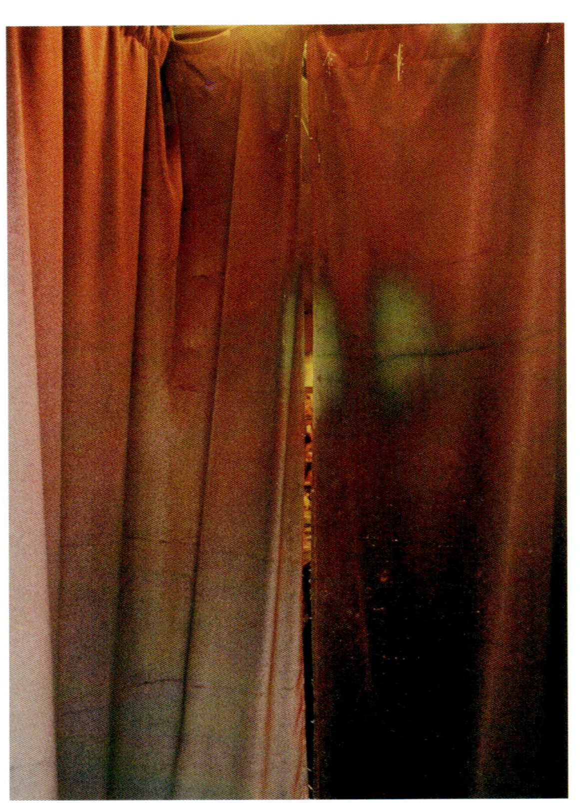

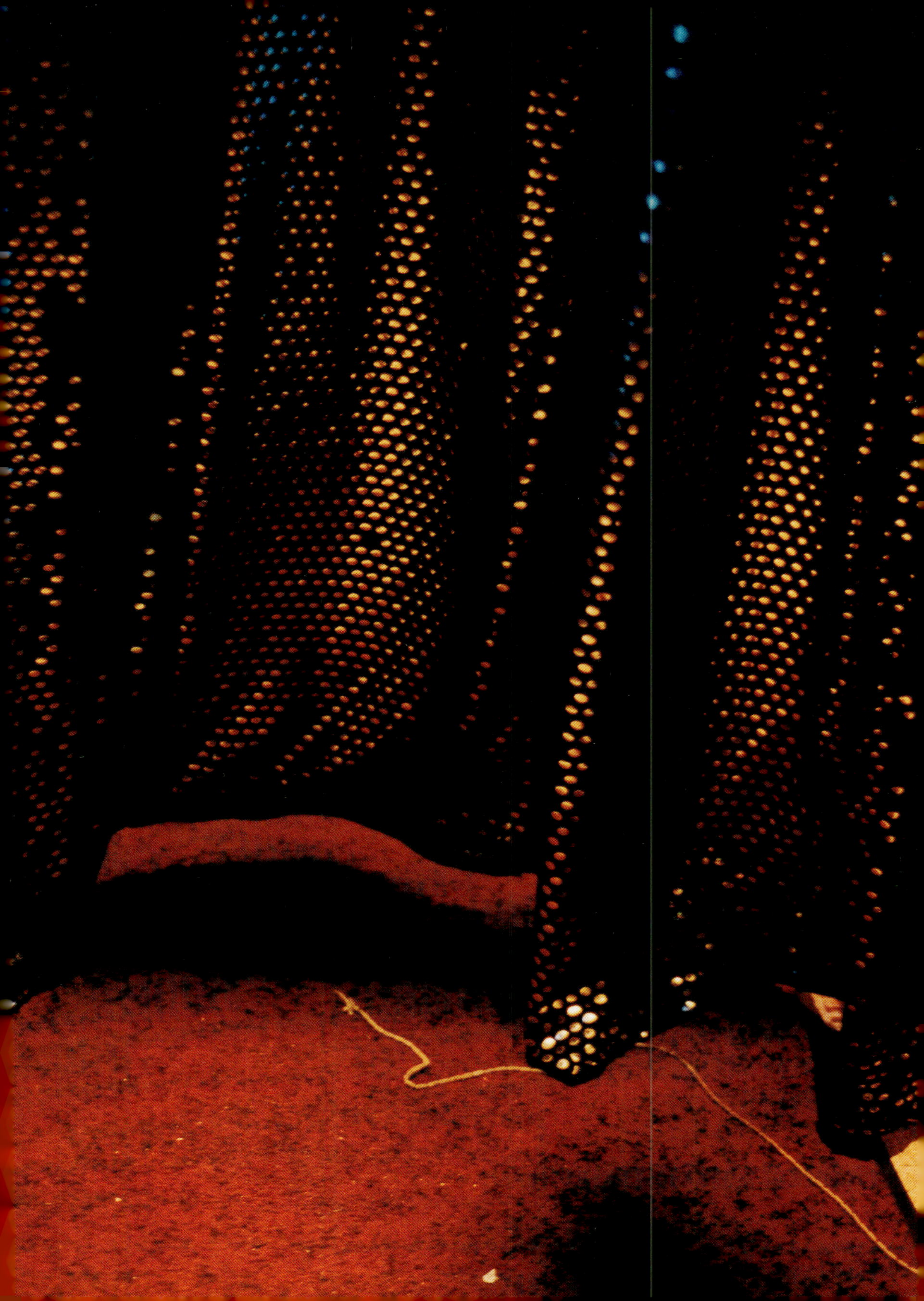

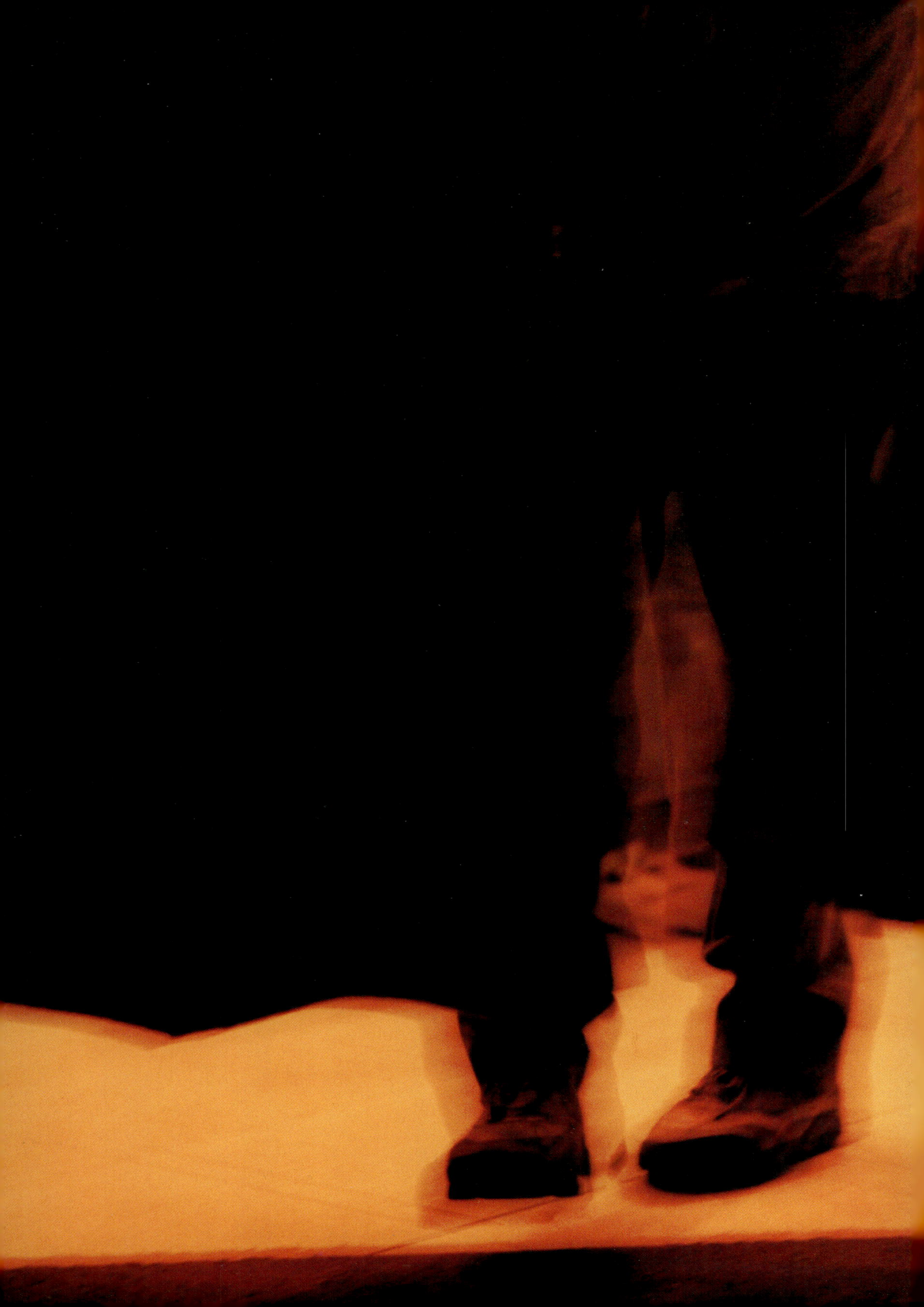

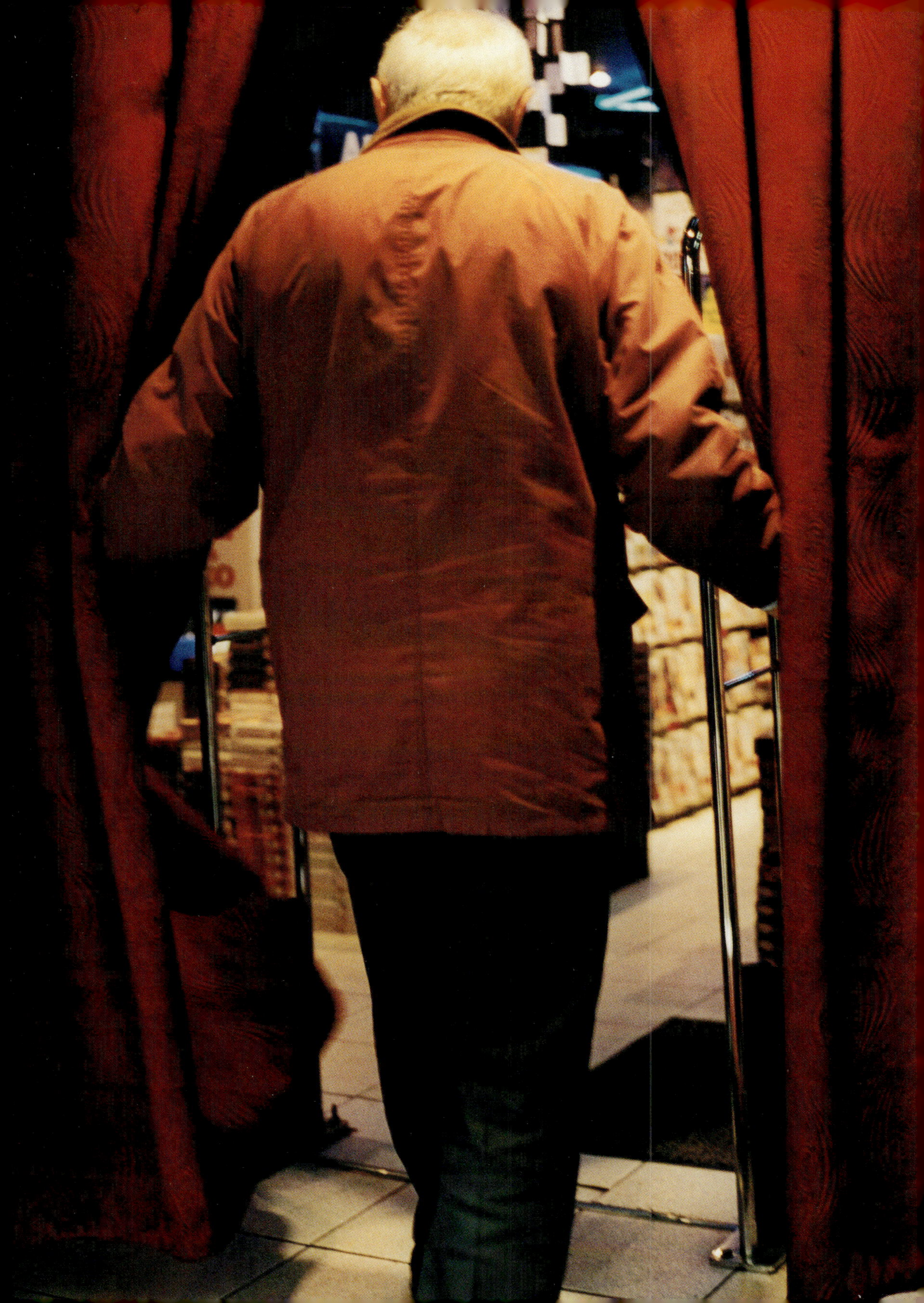

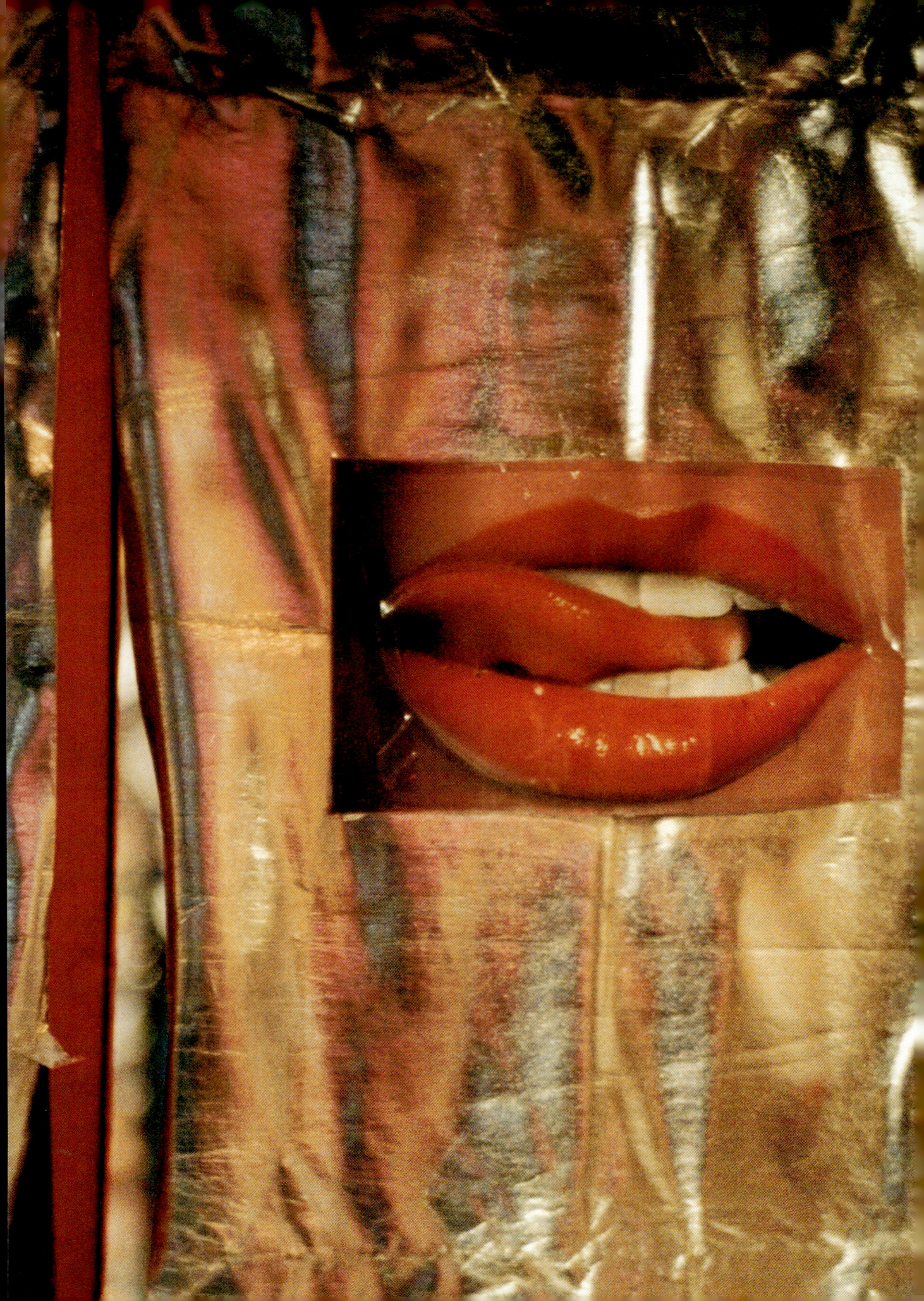

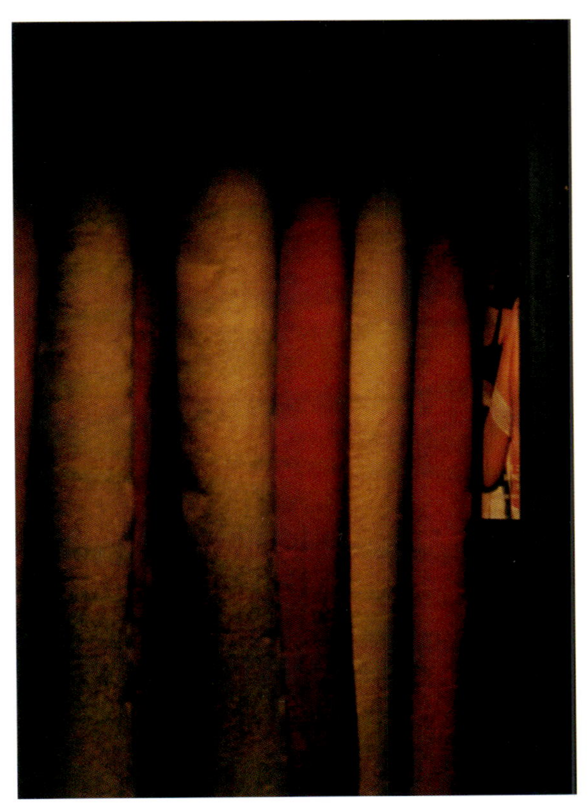

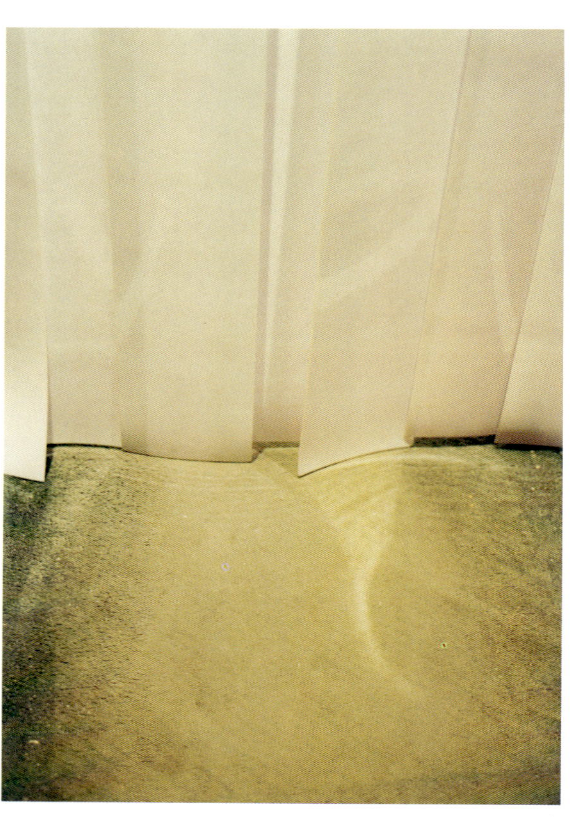

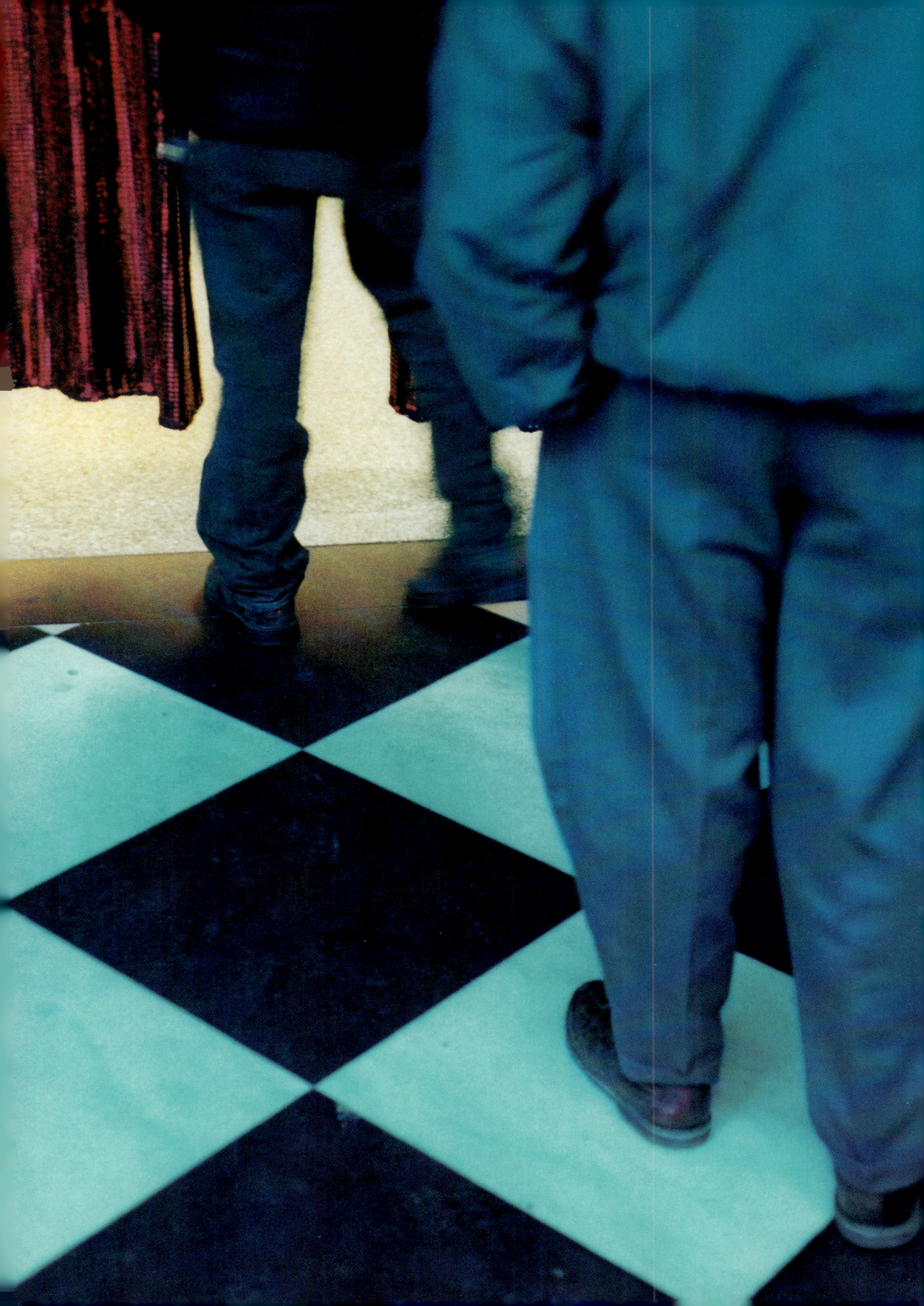

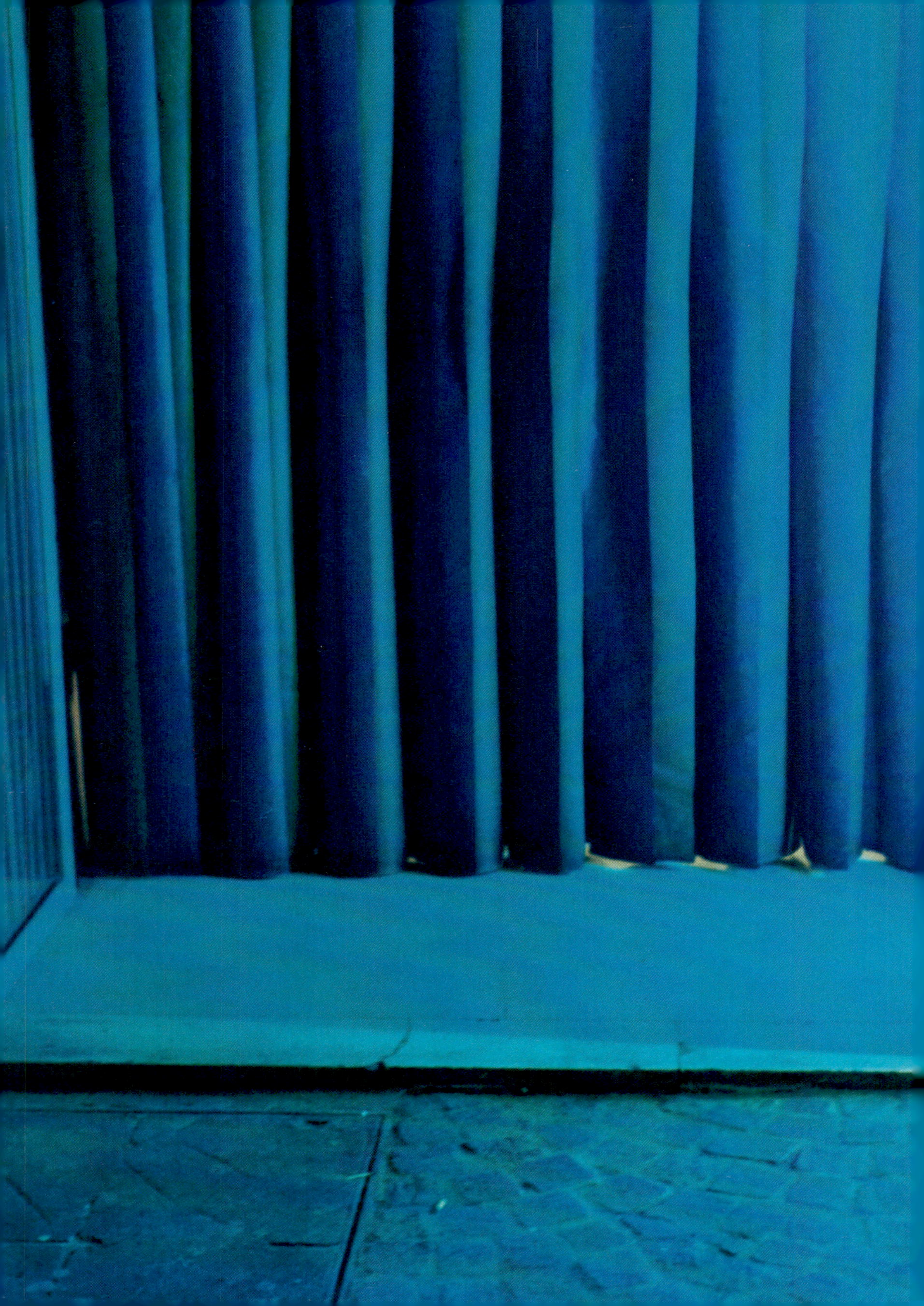

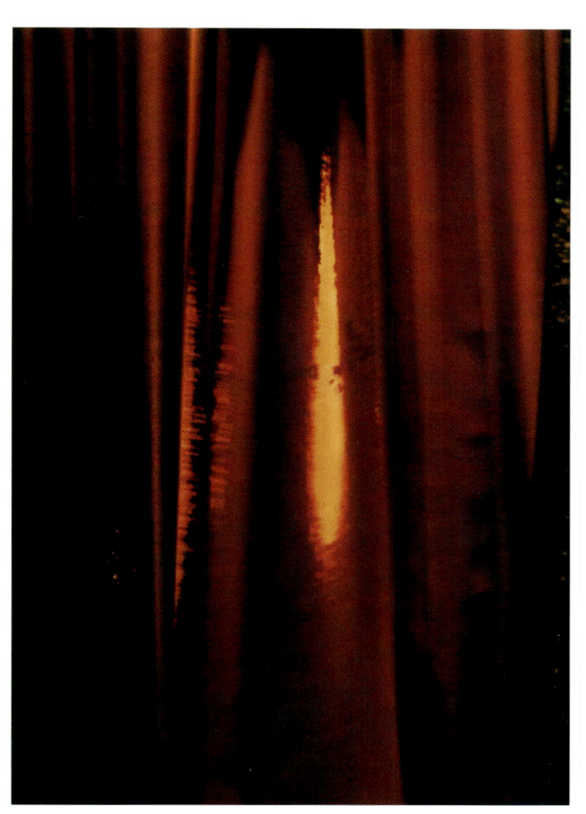

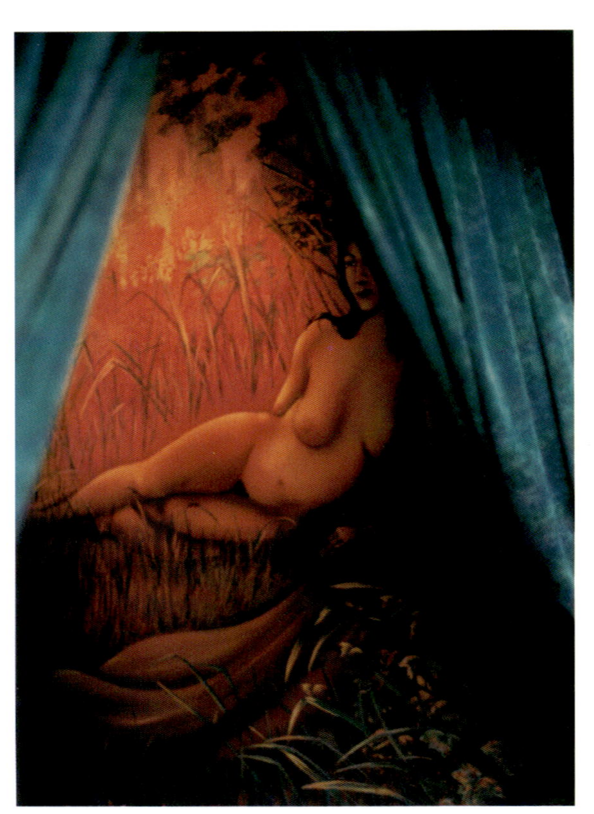

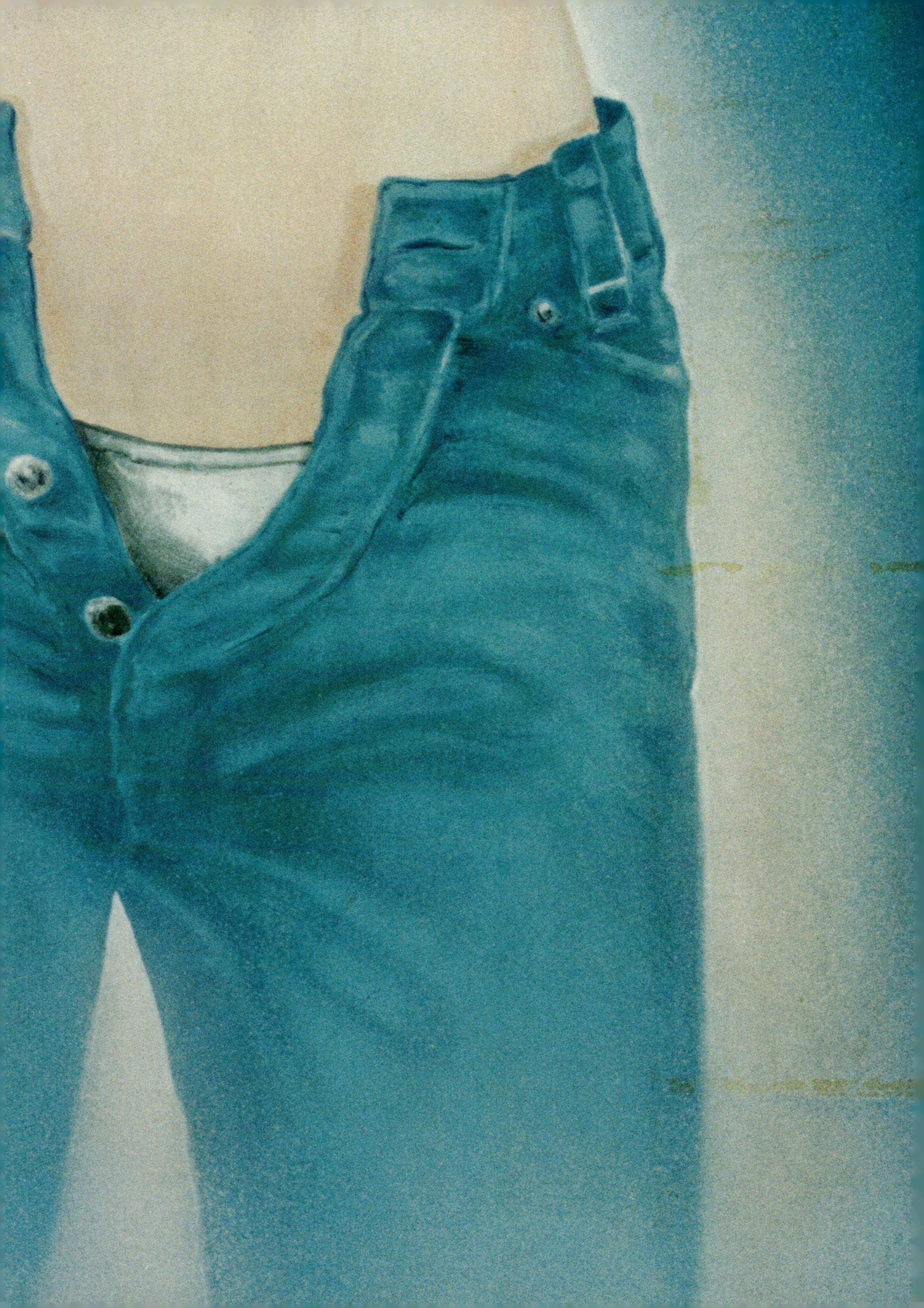

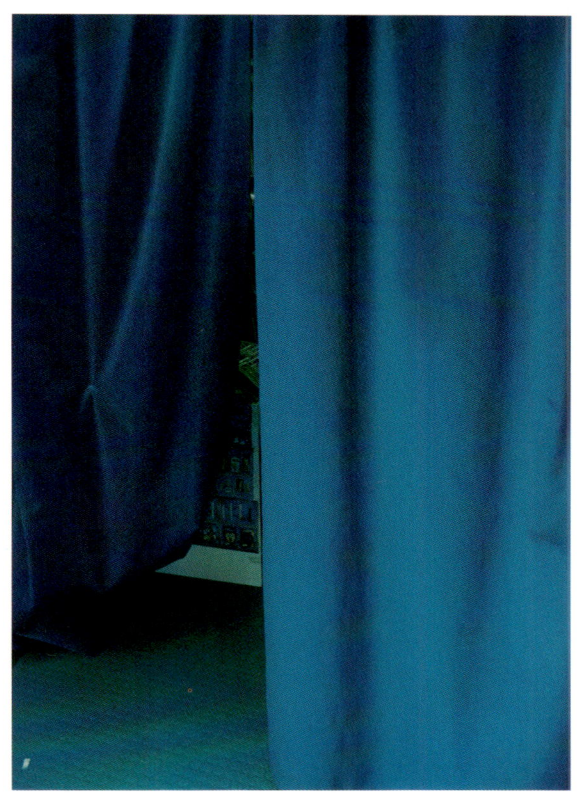

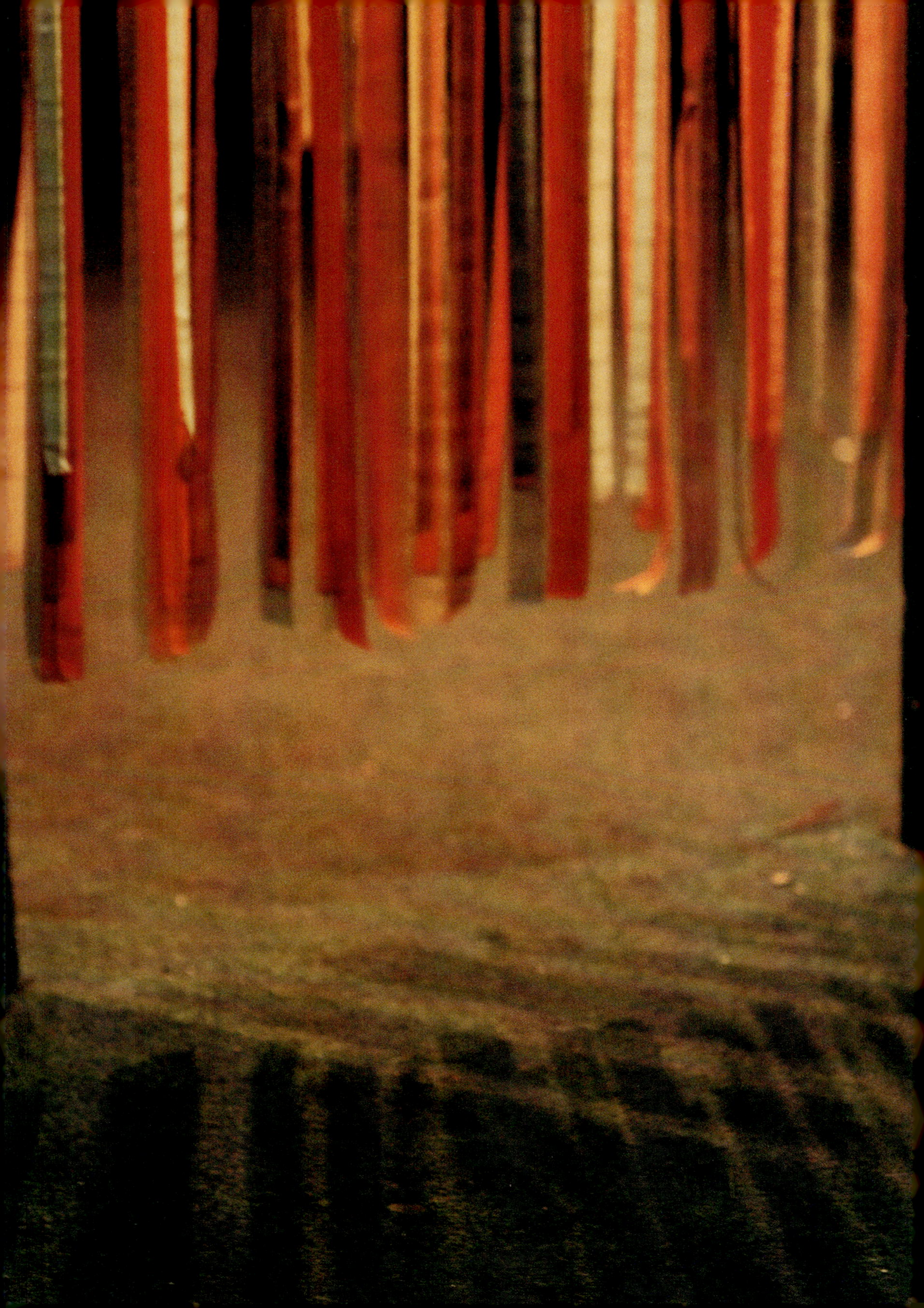

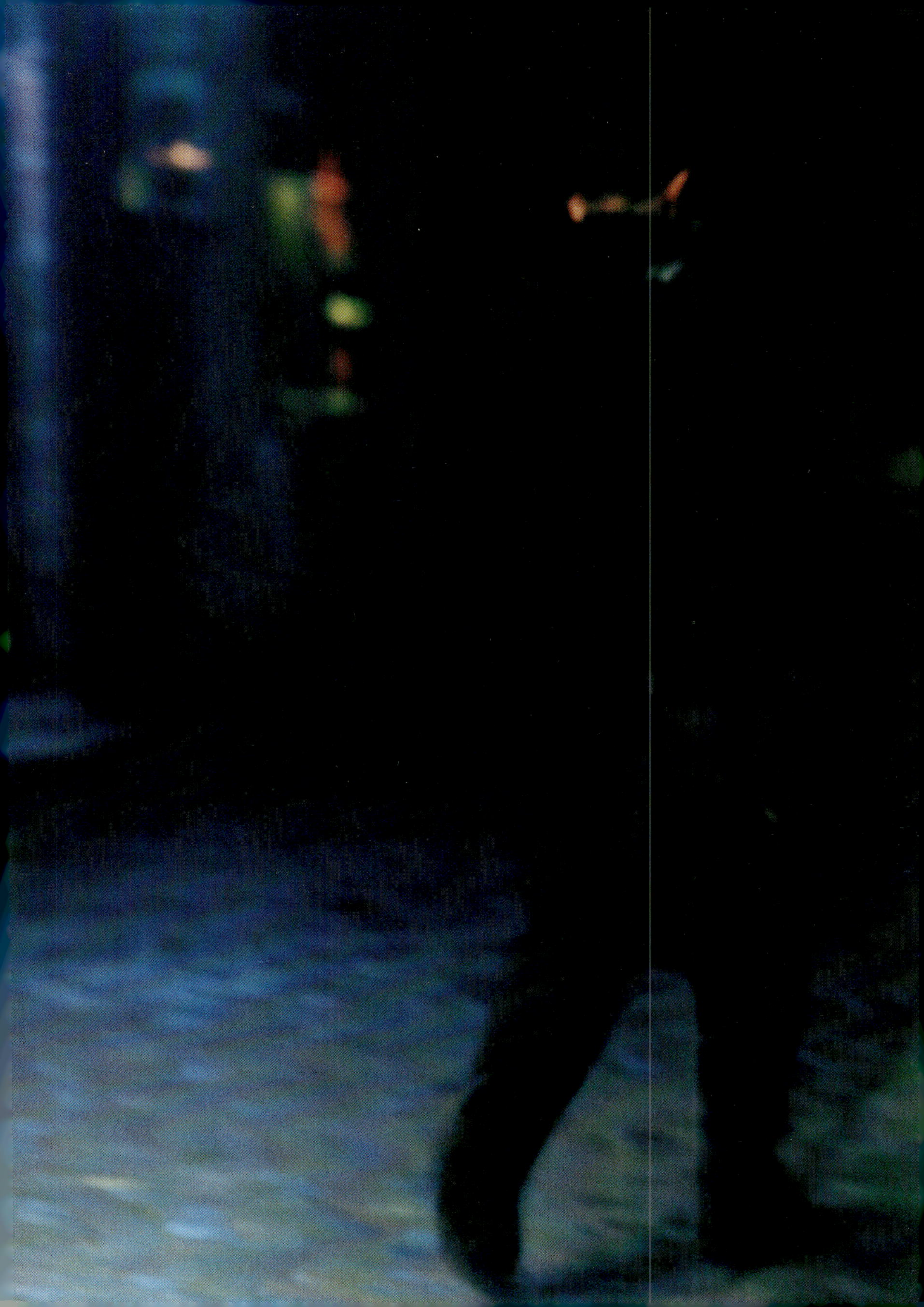

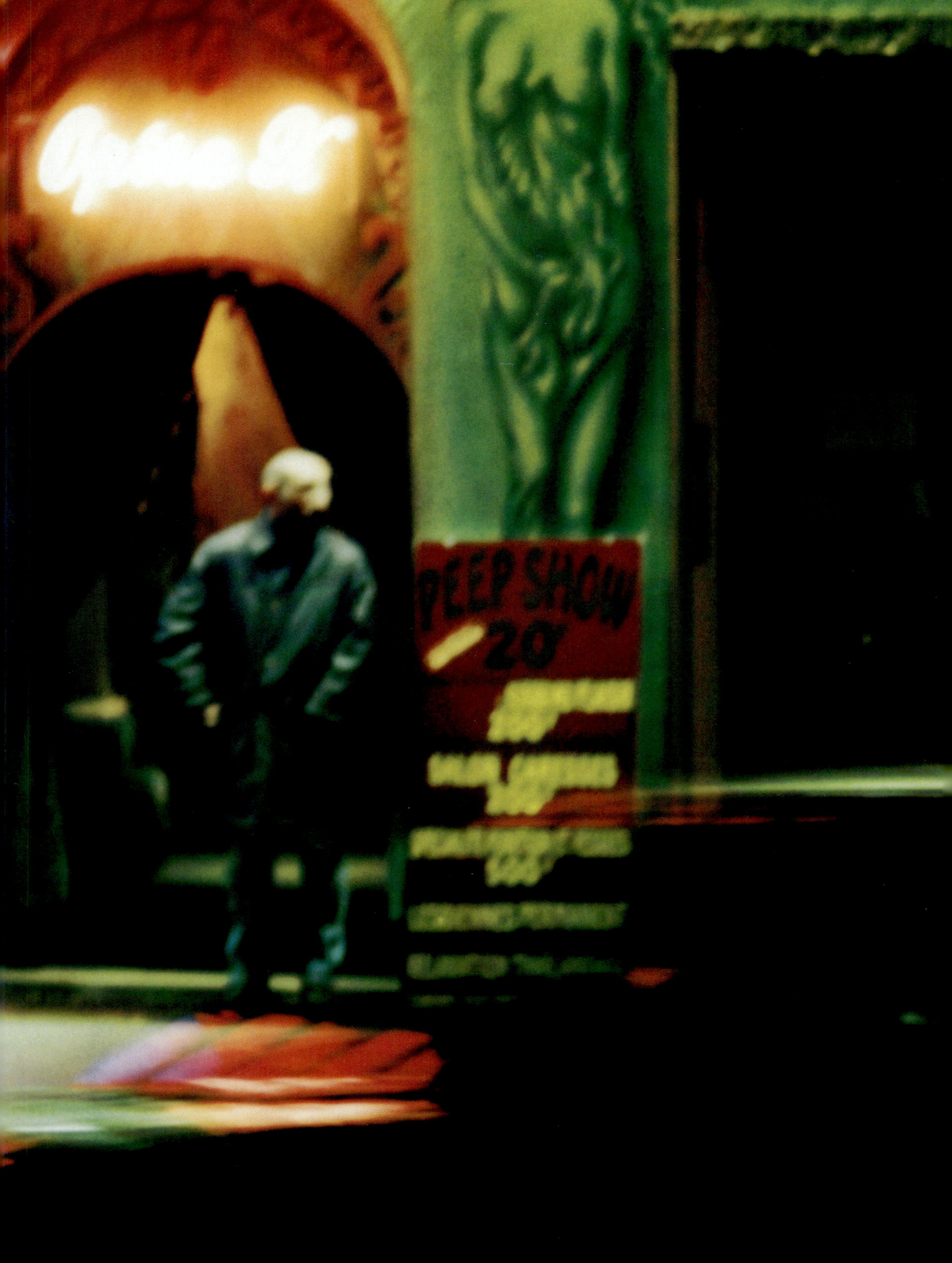
PEEP SHOW
20

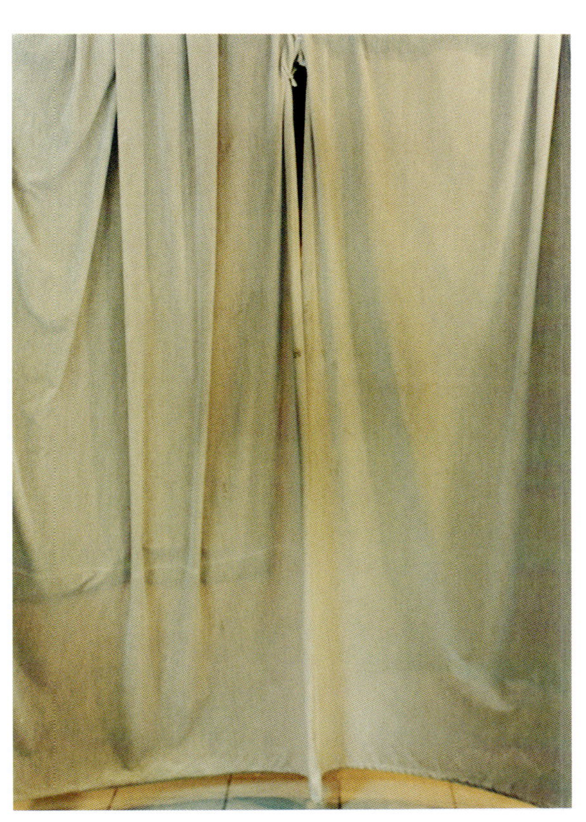

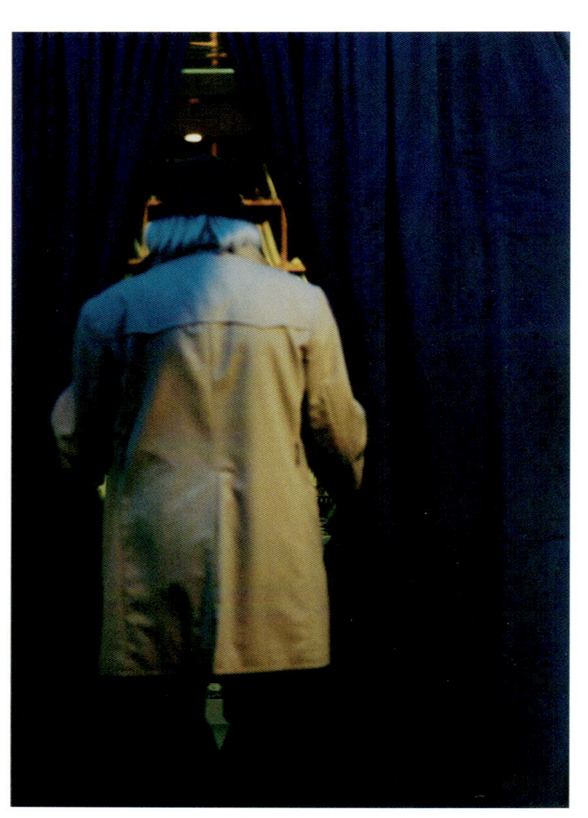

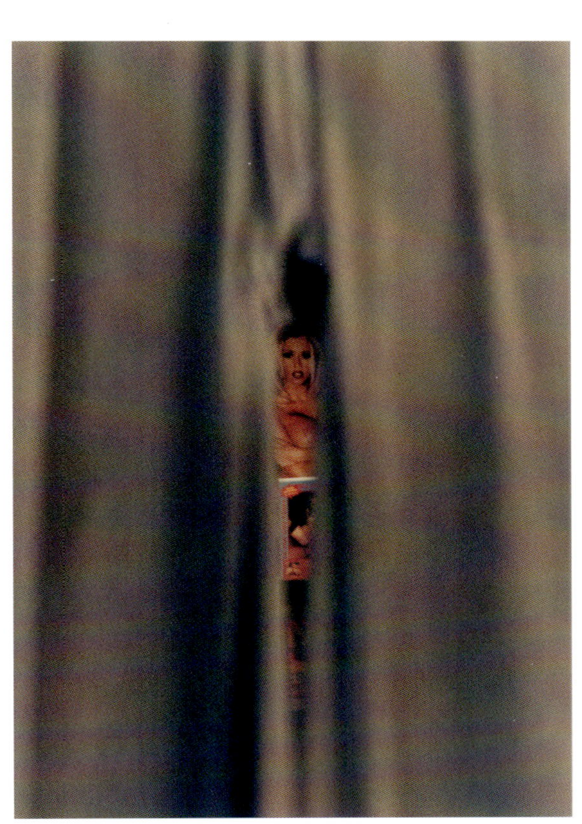

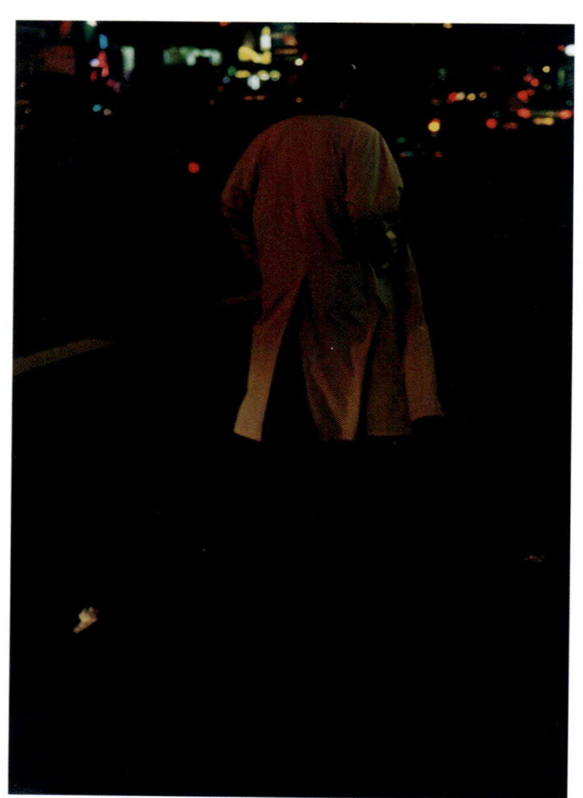

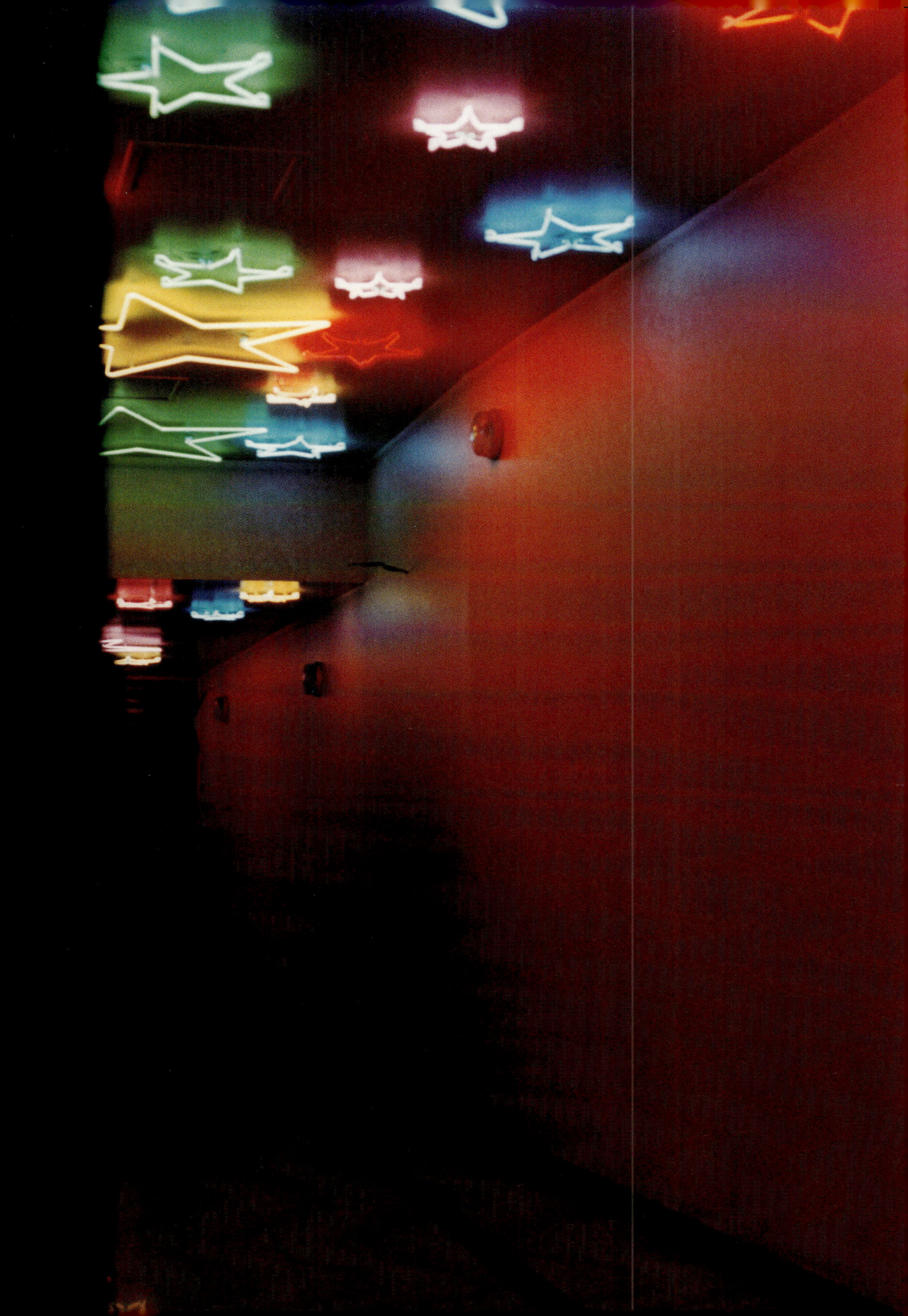

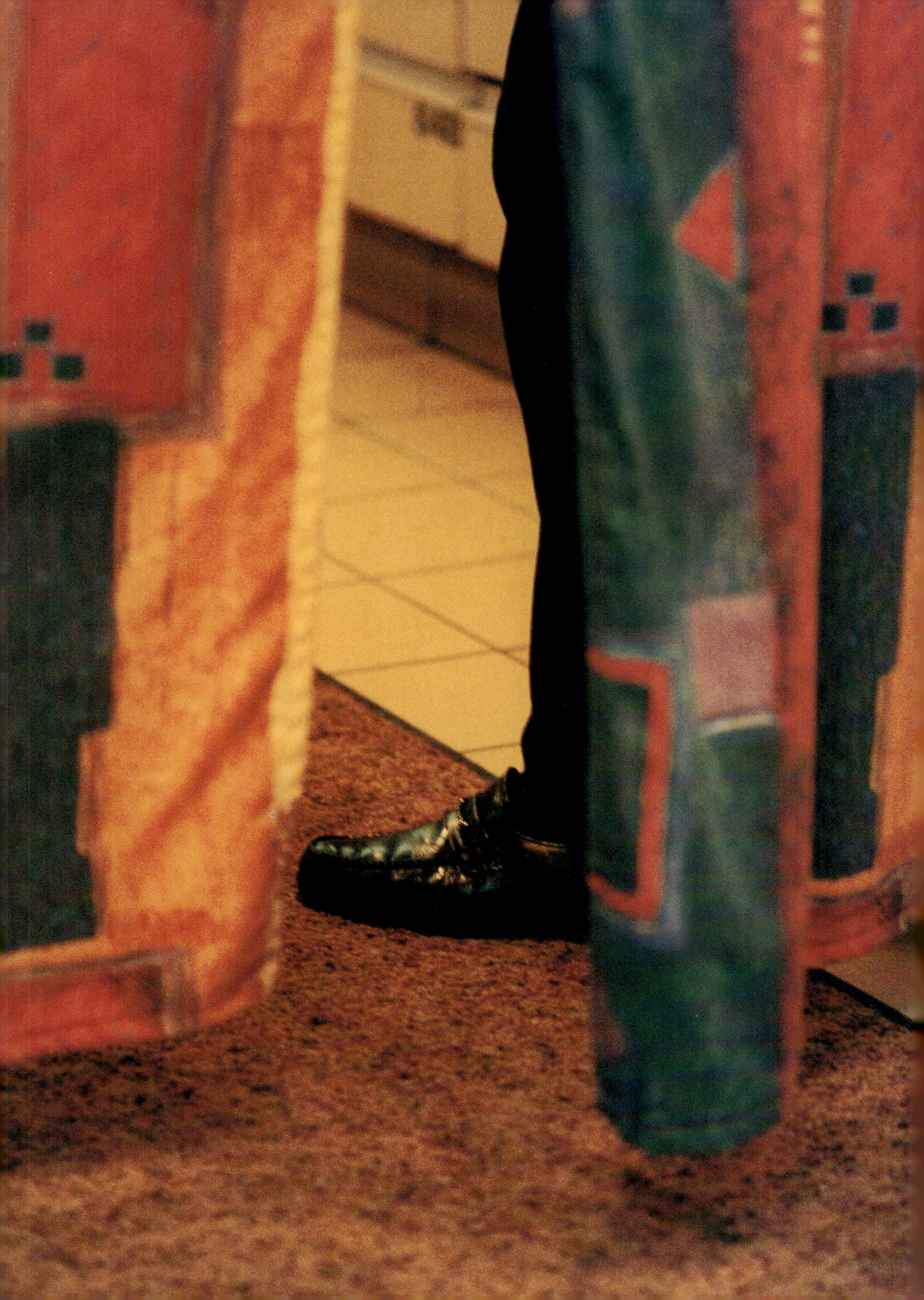

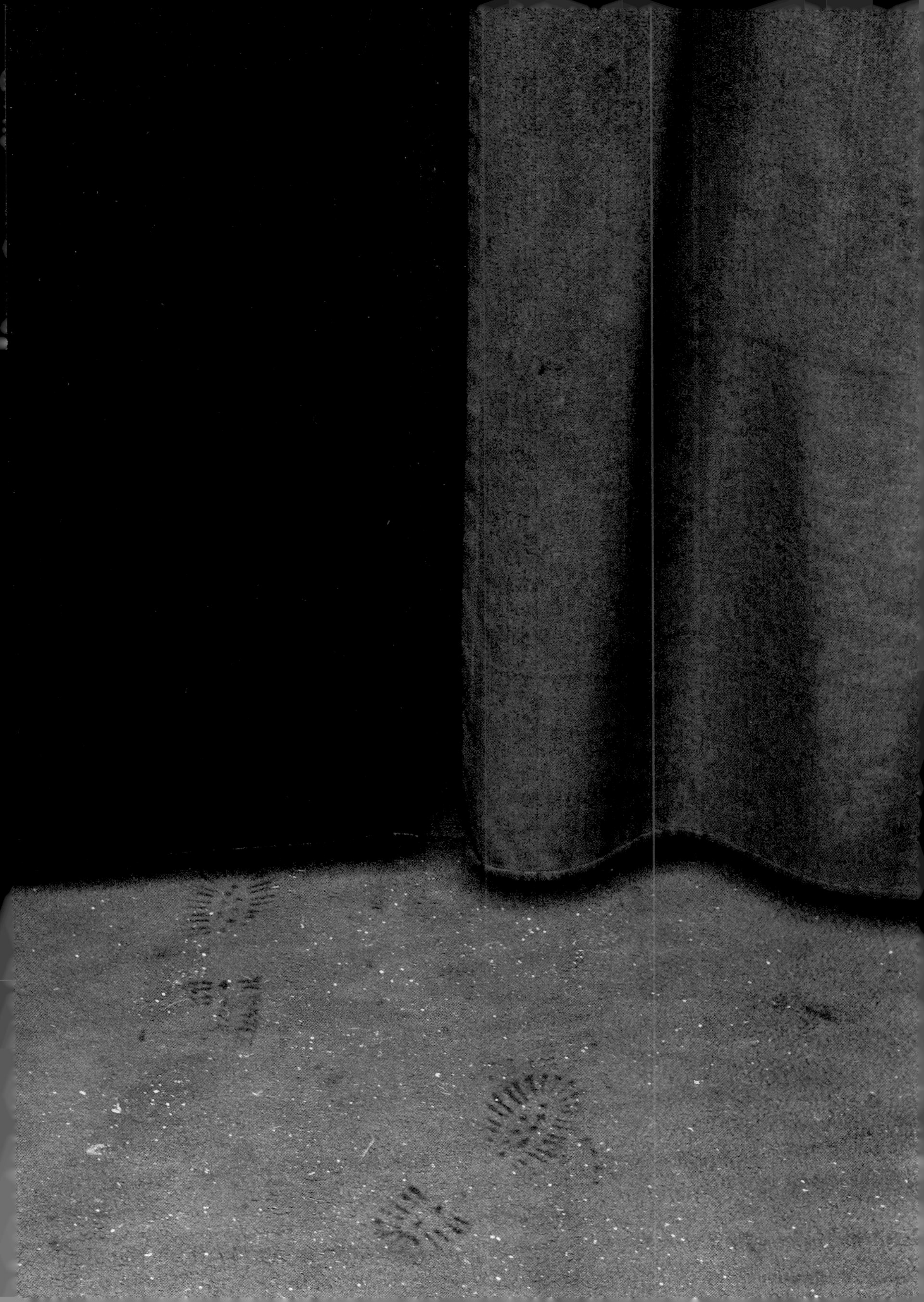

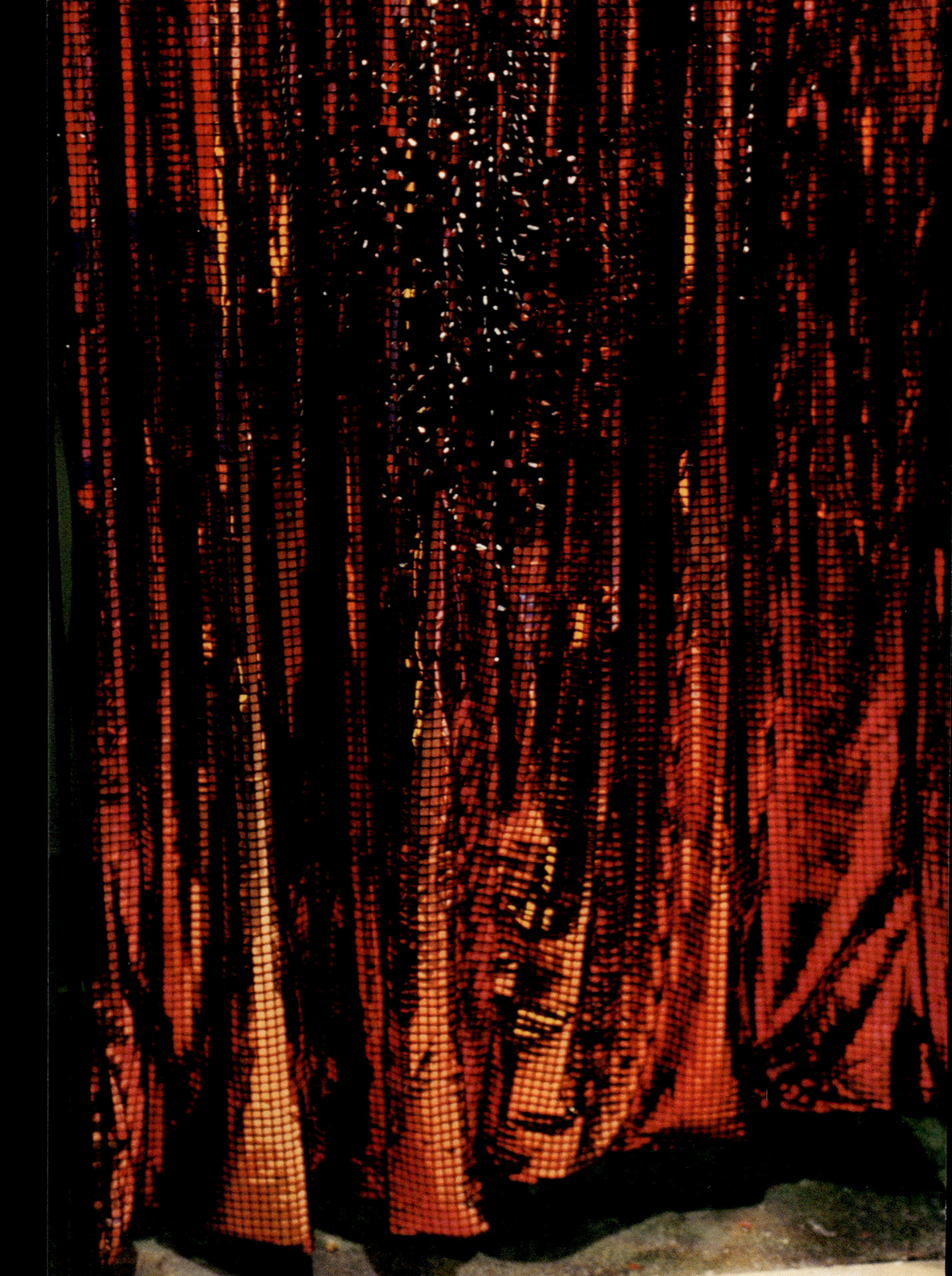

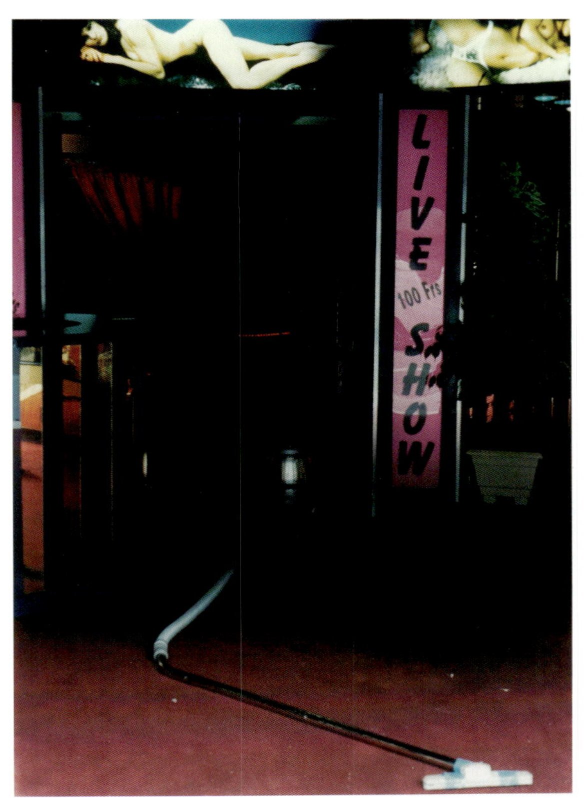
LIVE
100 Frs
SHOW

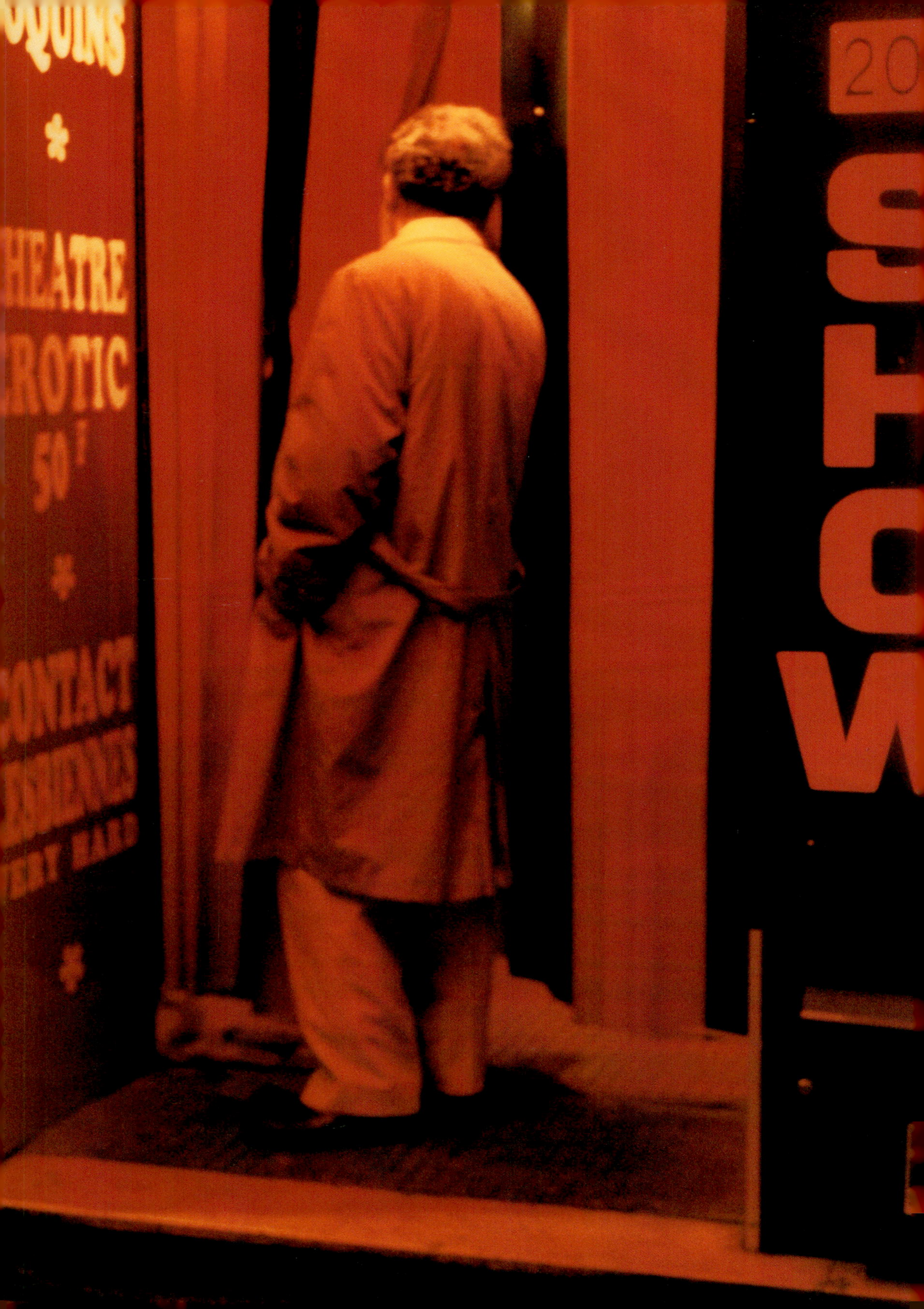
EROTIC
50 F
CONTACT
20
SHOW

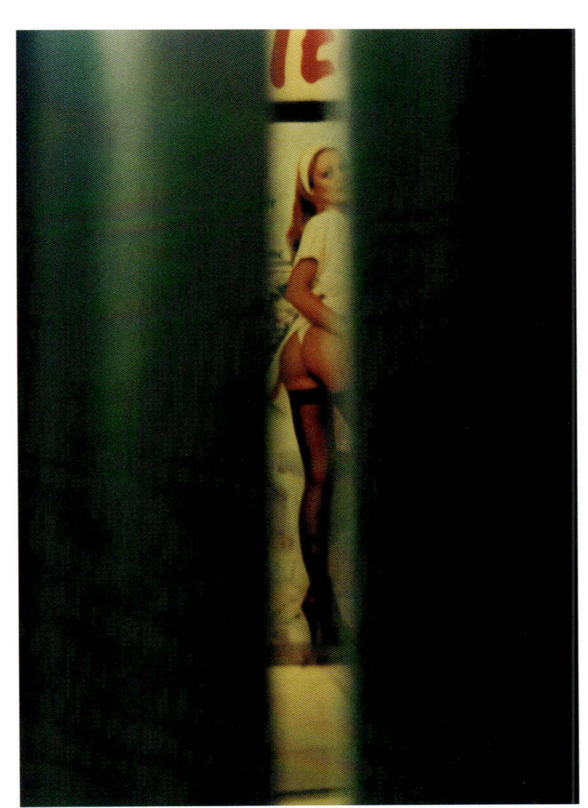

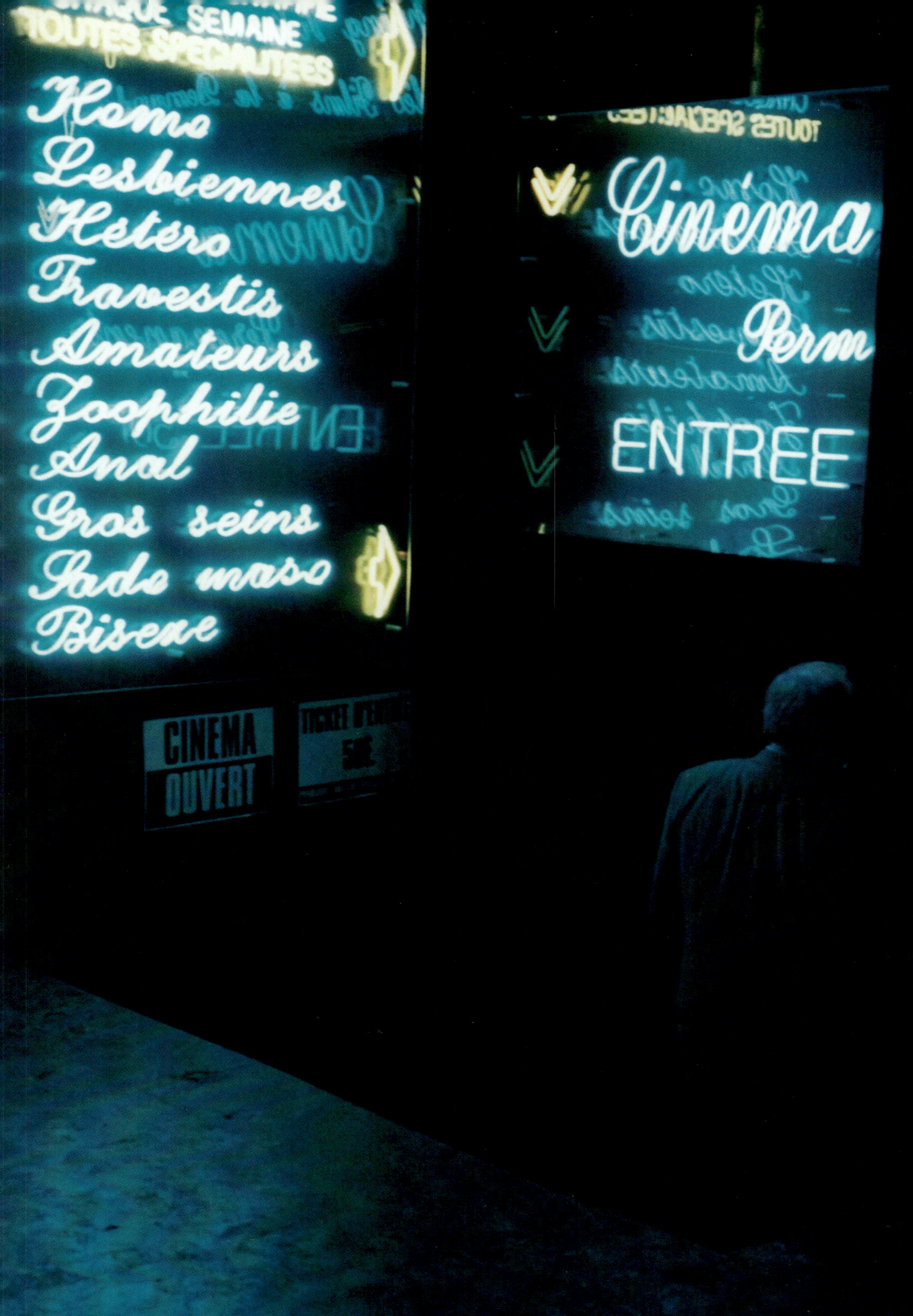
SEMAINE
TOUTES SPECIALITEES
Homo
Lesbiennes
Hétéro
Travestis
Amateurs
Zoophilie
Anal
Gros seins
Sado maso
Bisexe
TOUTES SPECIALITEES
Cinéma
Perm
ENTREE
CINEMA
OUVERT

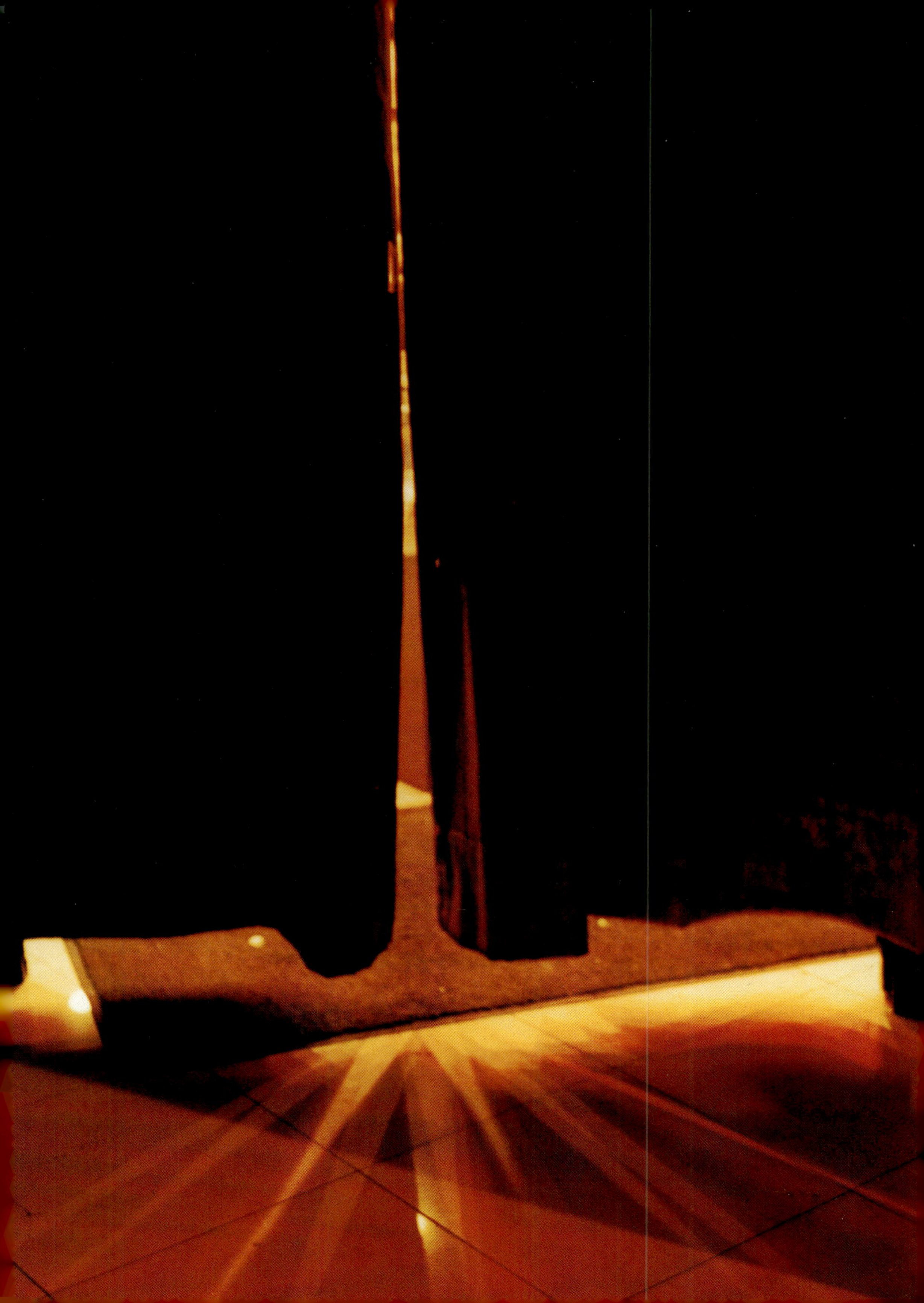

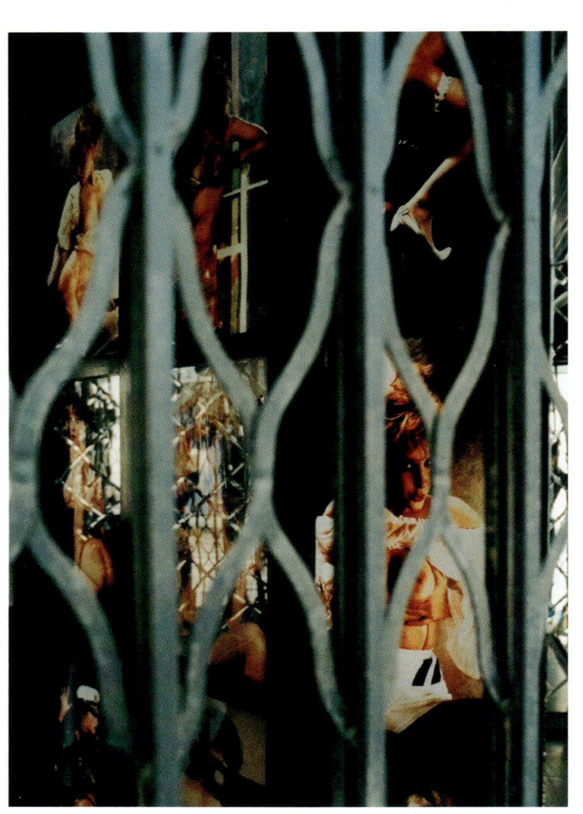

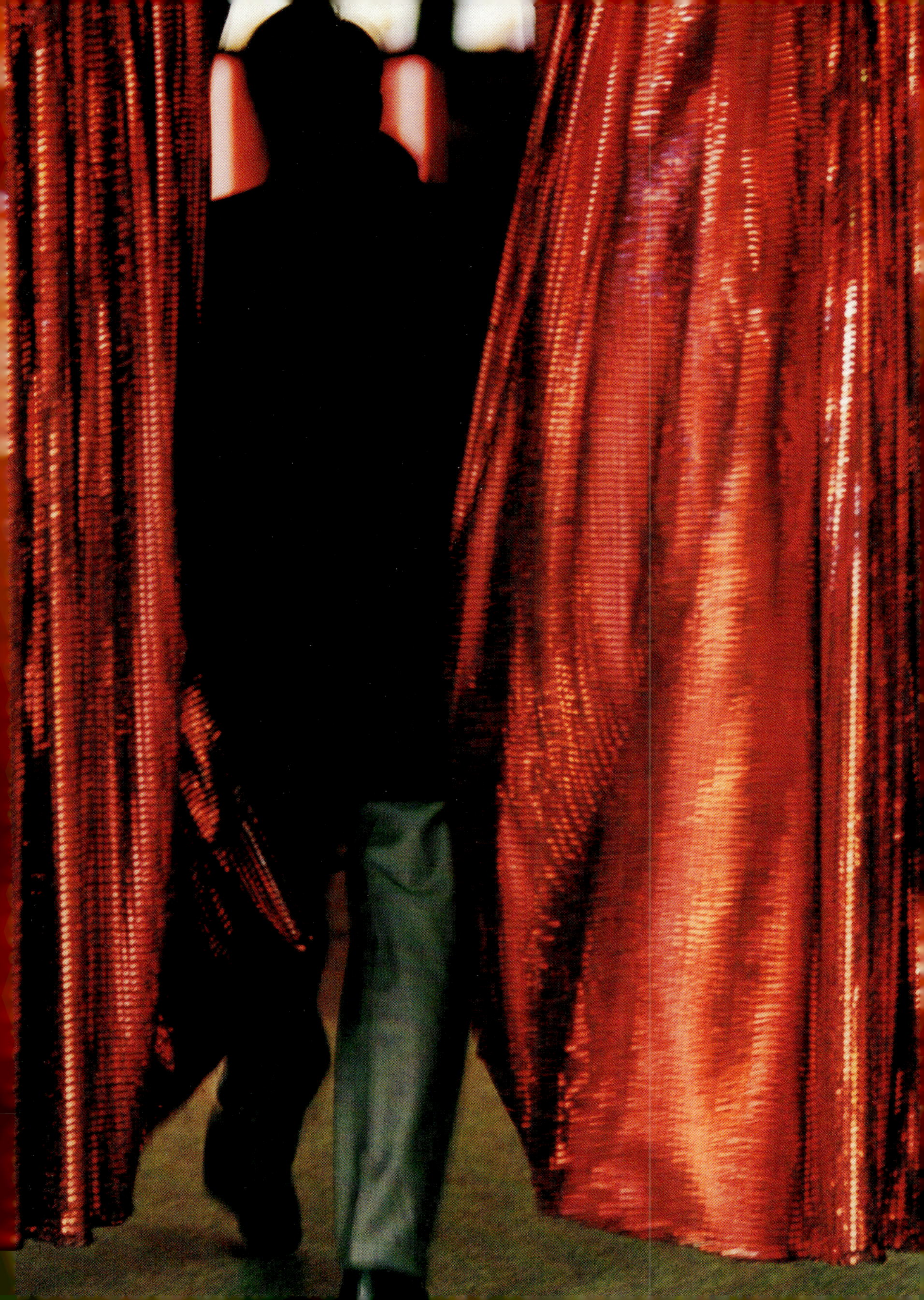

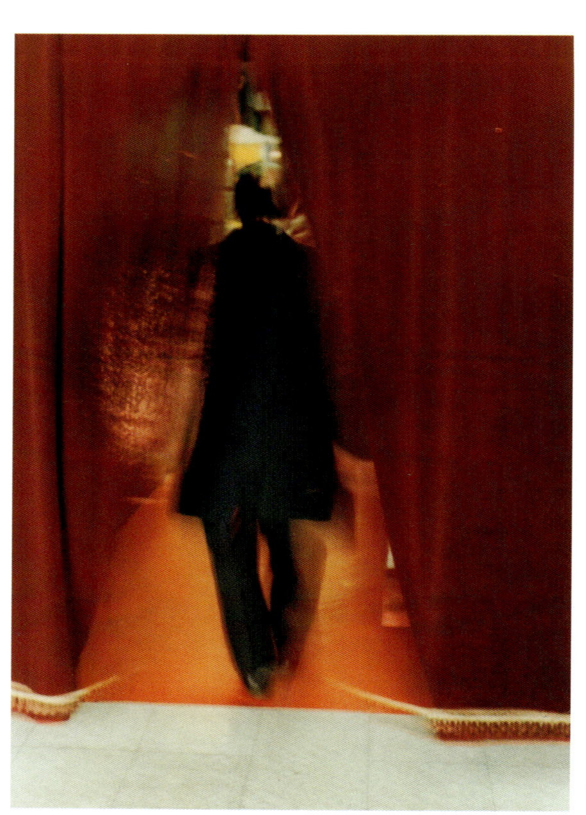

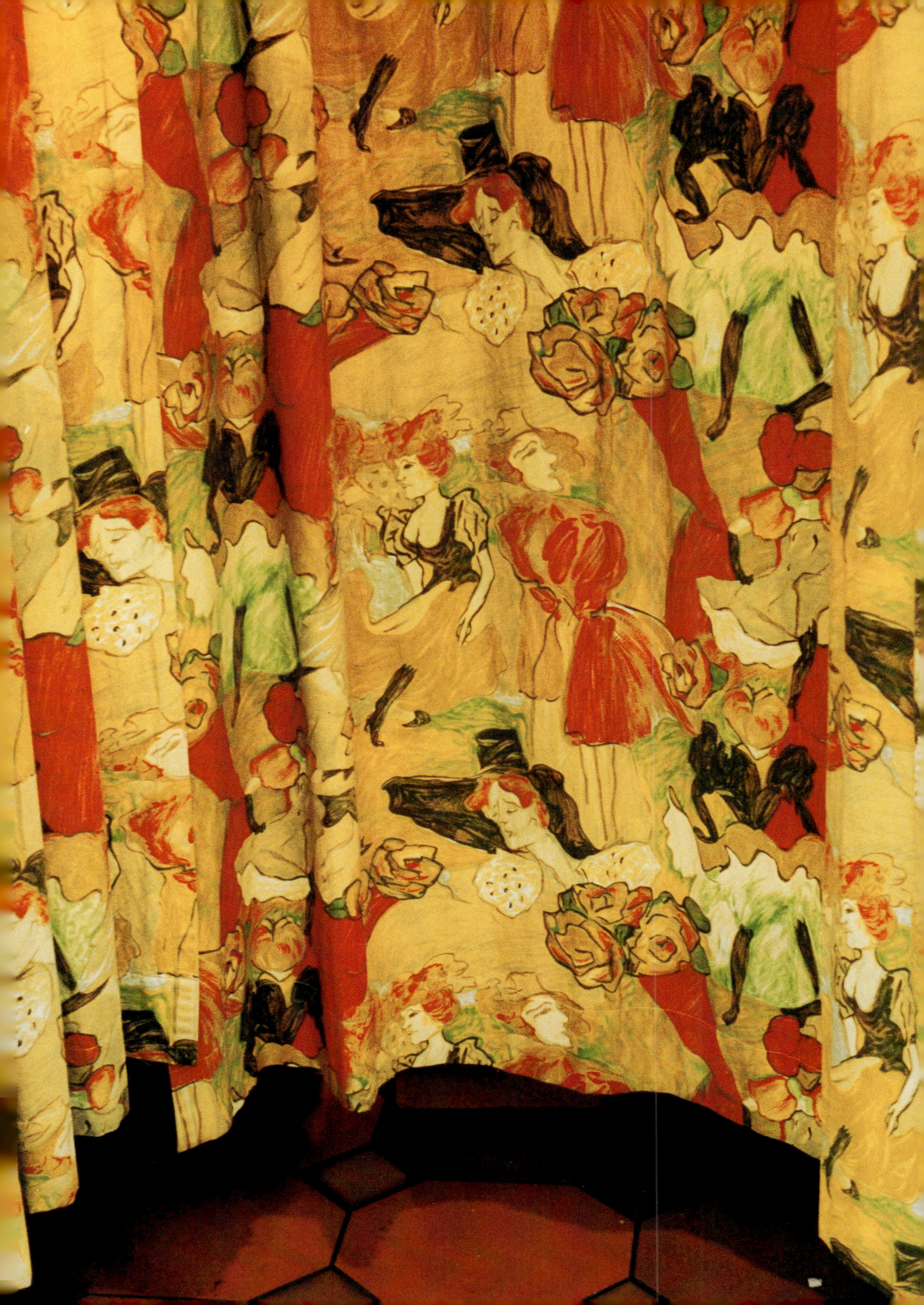

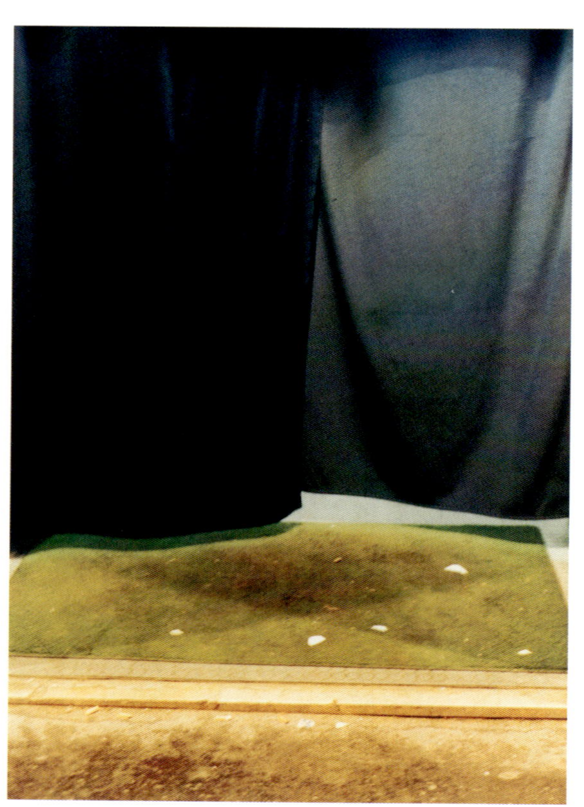

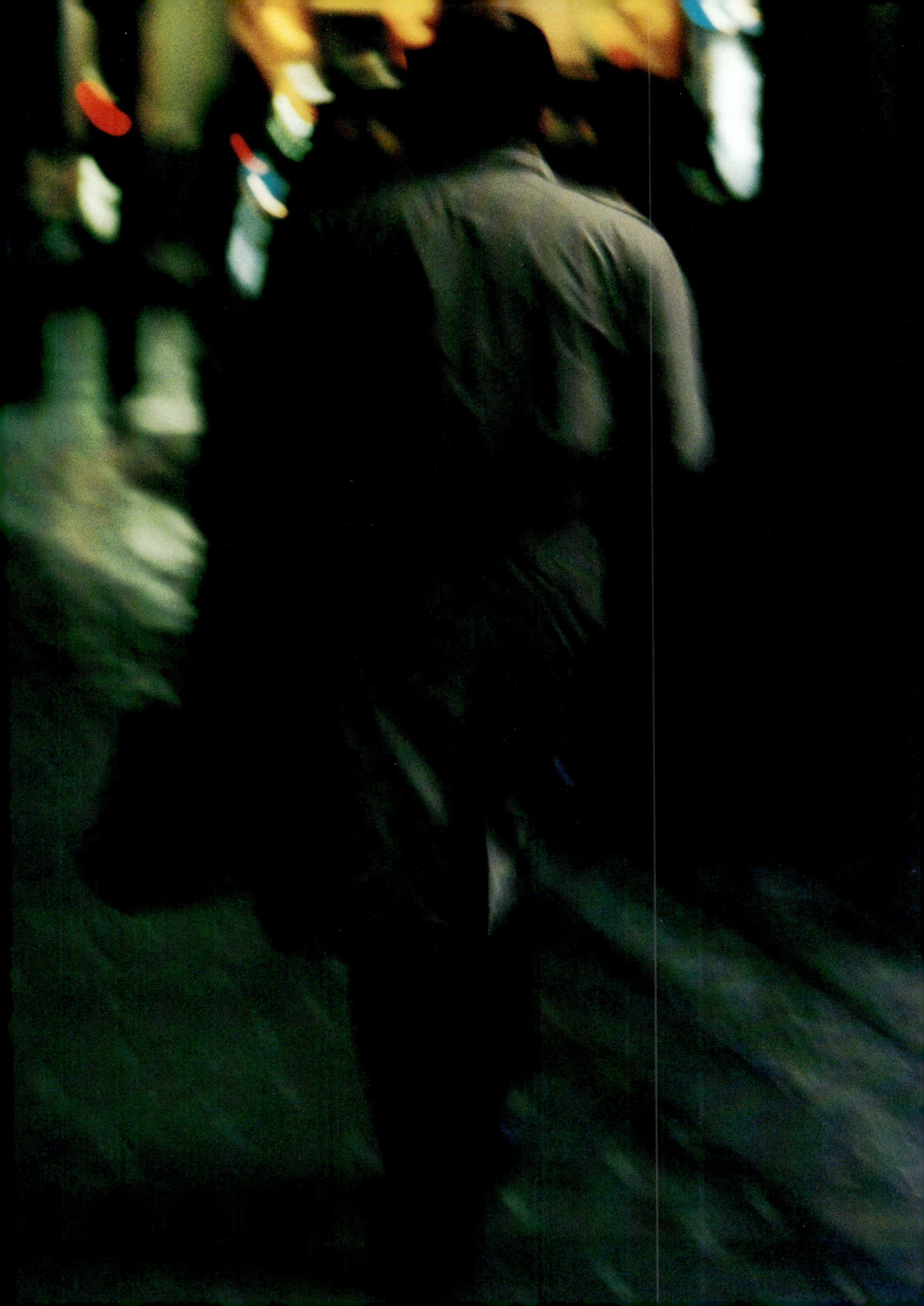

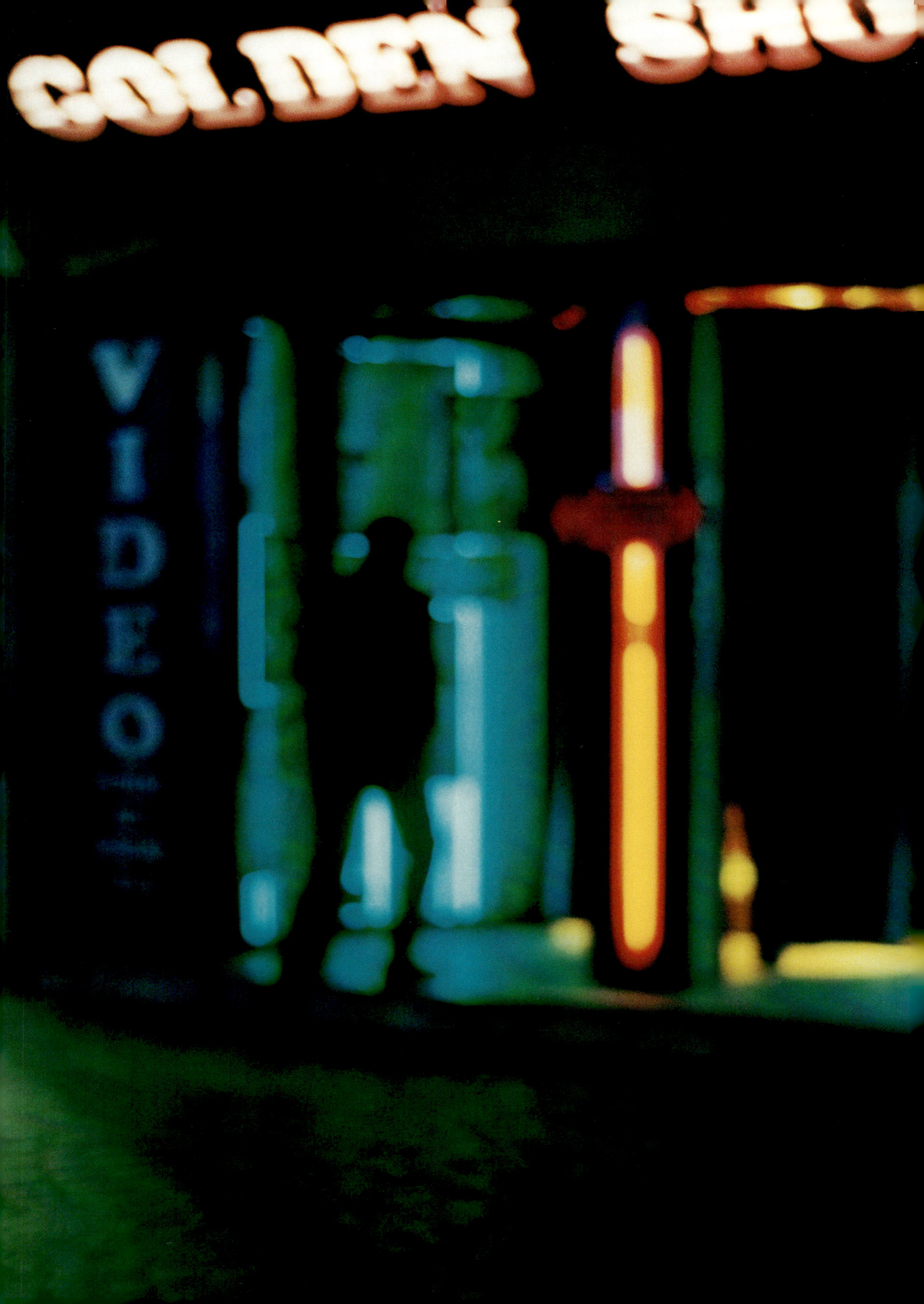
GOLDEN
VIDEO

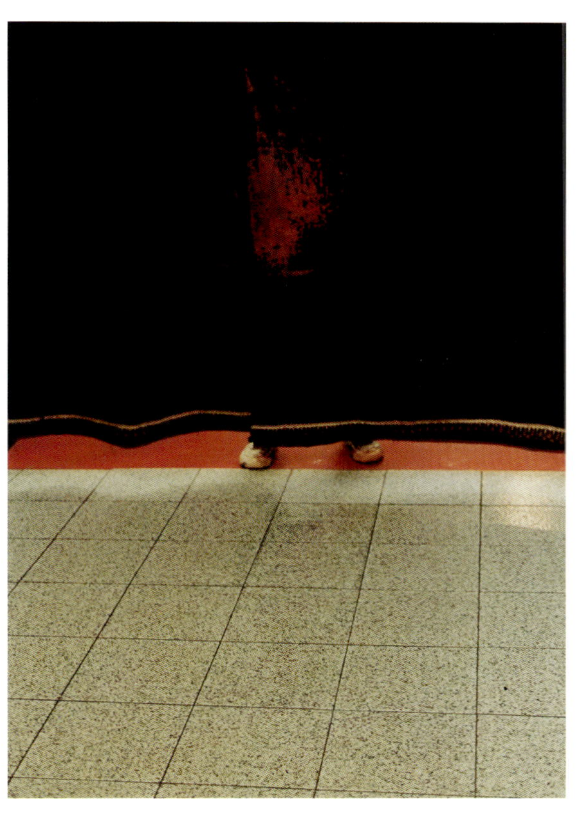

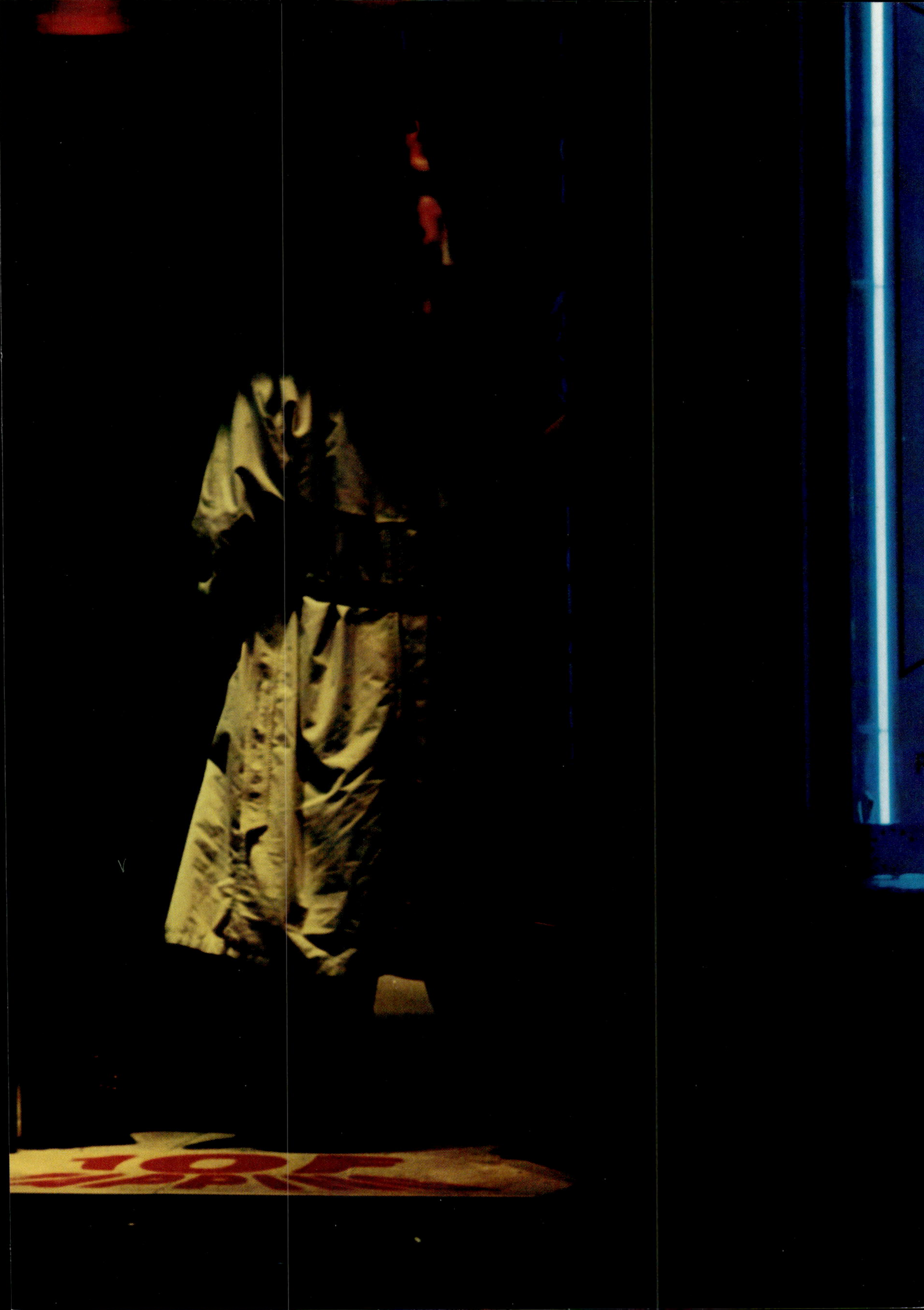

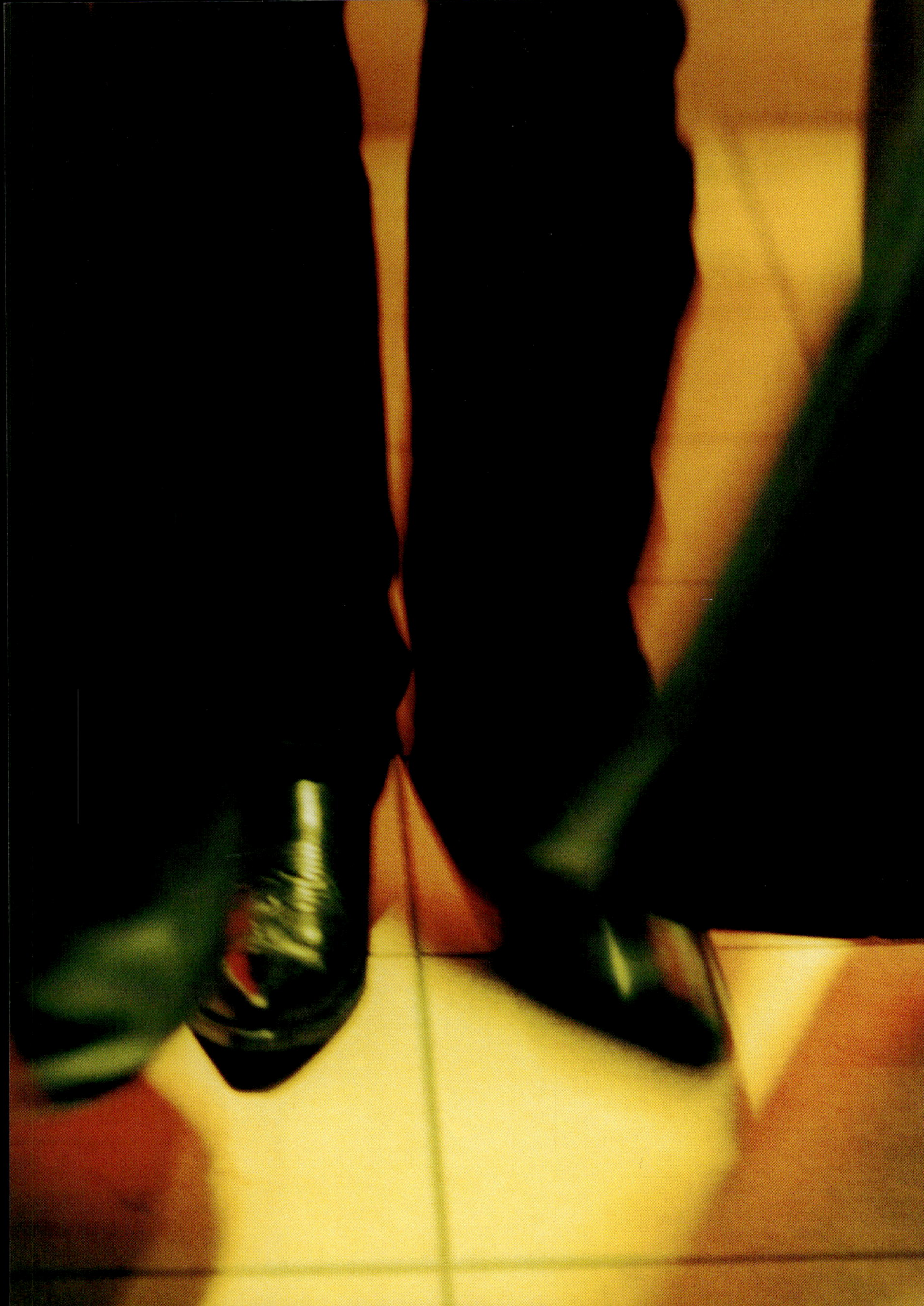

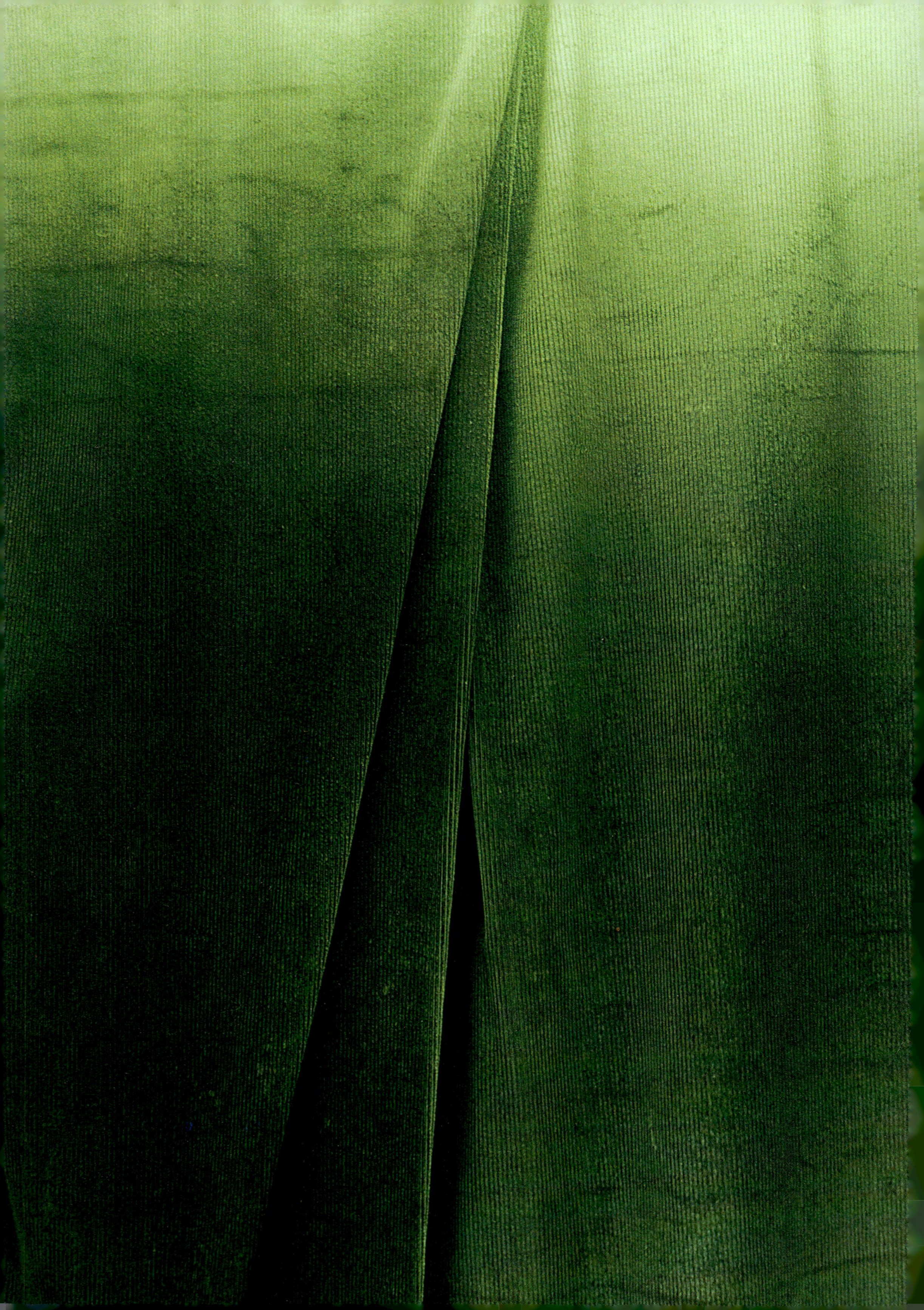

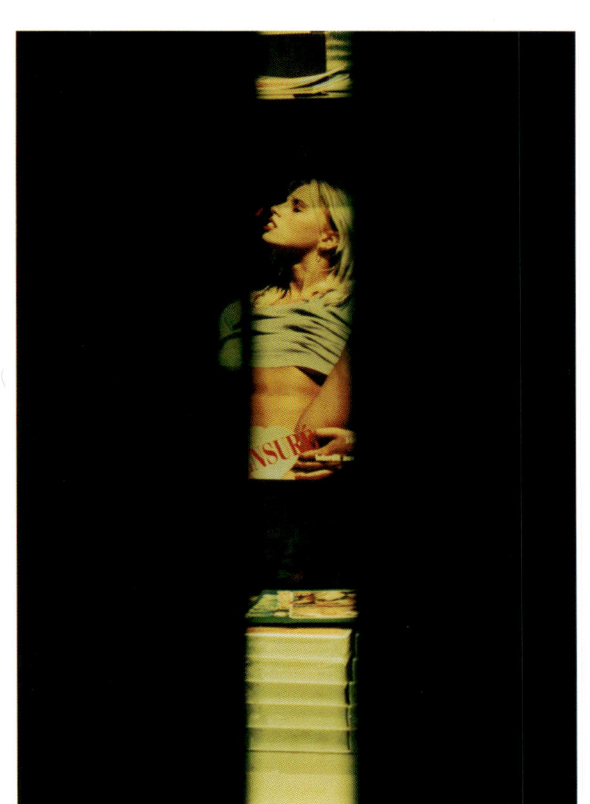

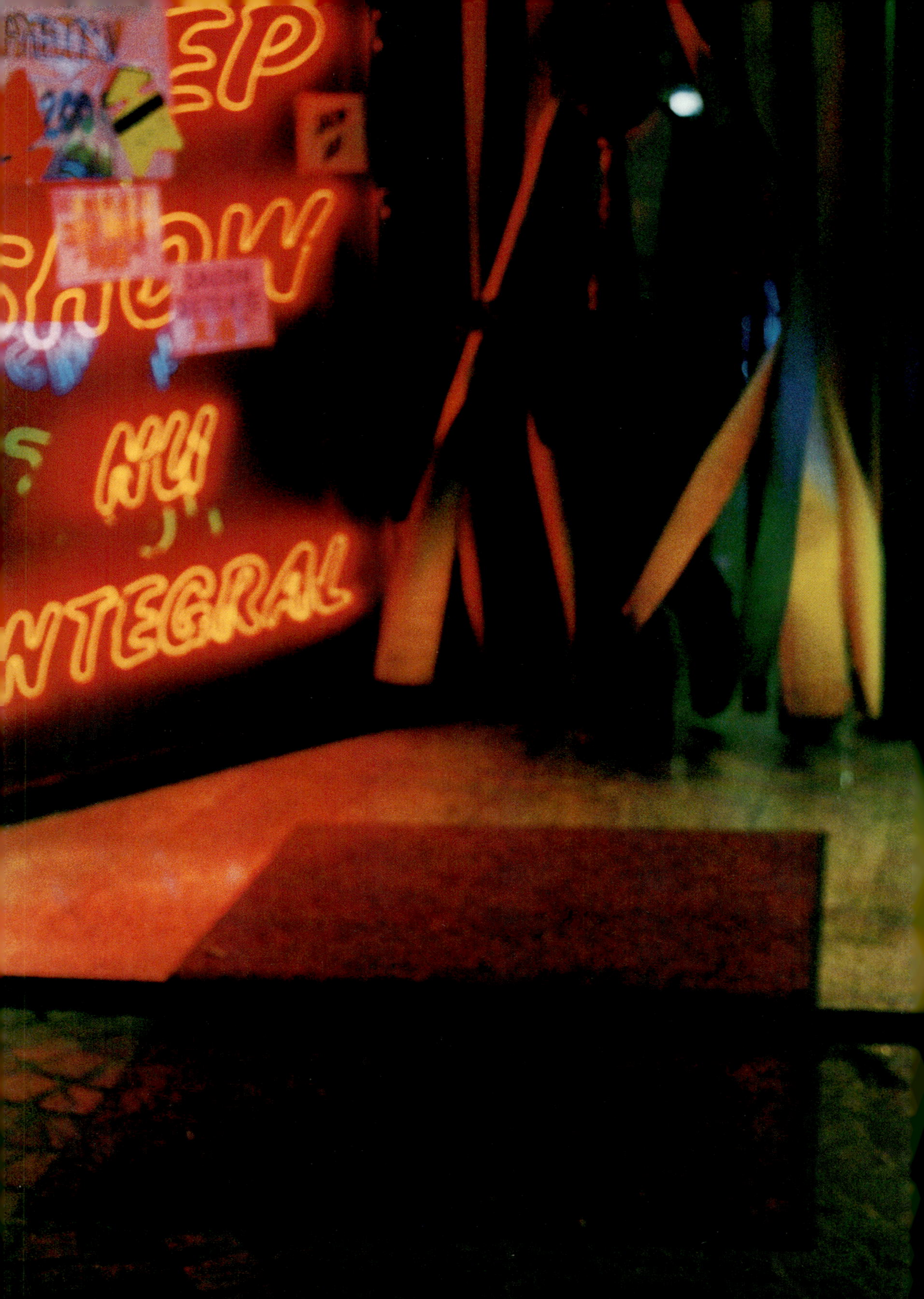
NU
NTEGRAL

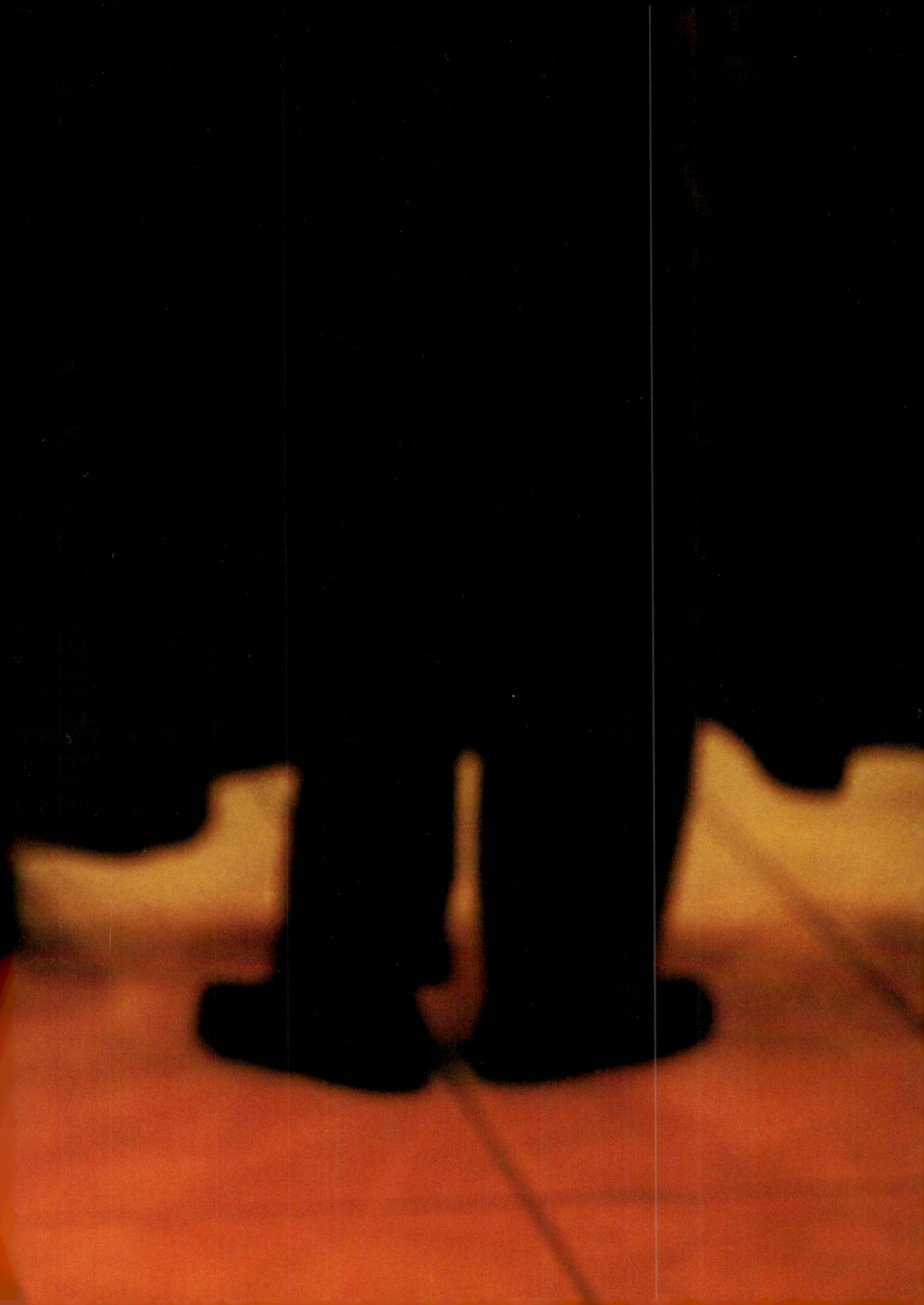

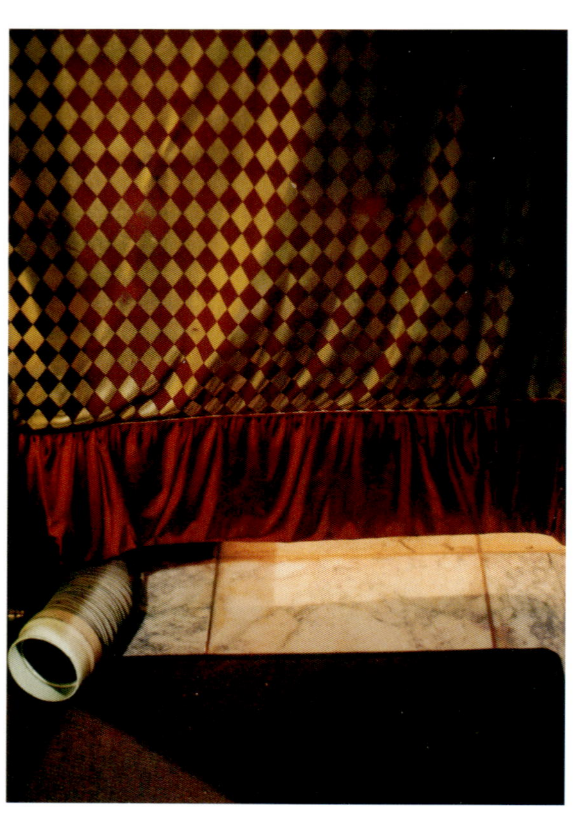

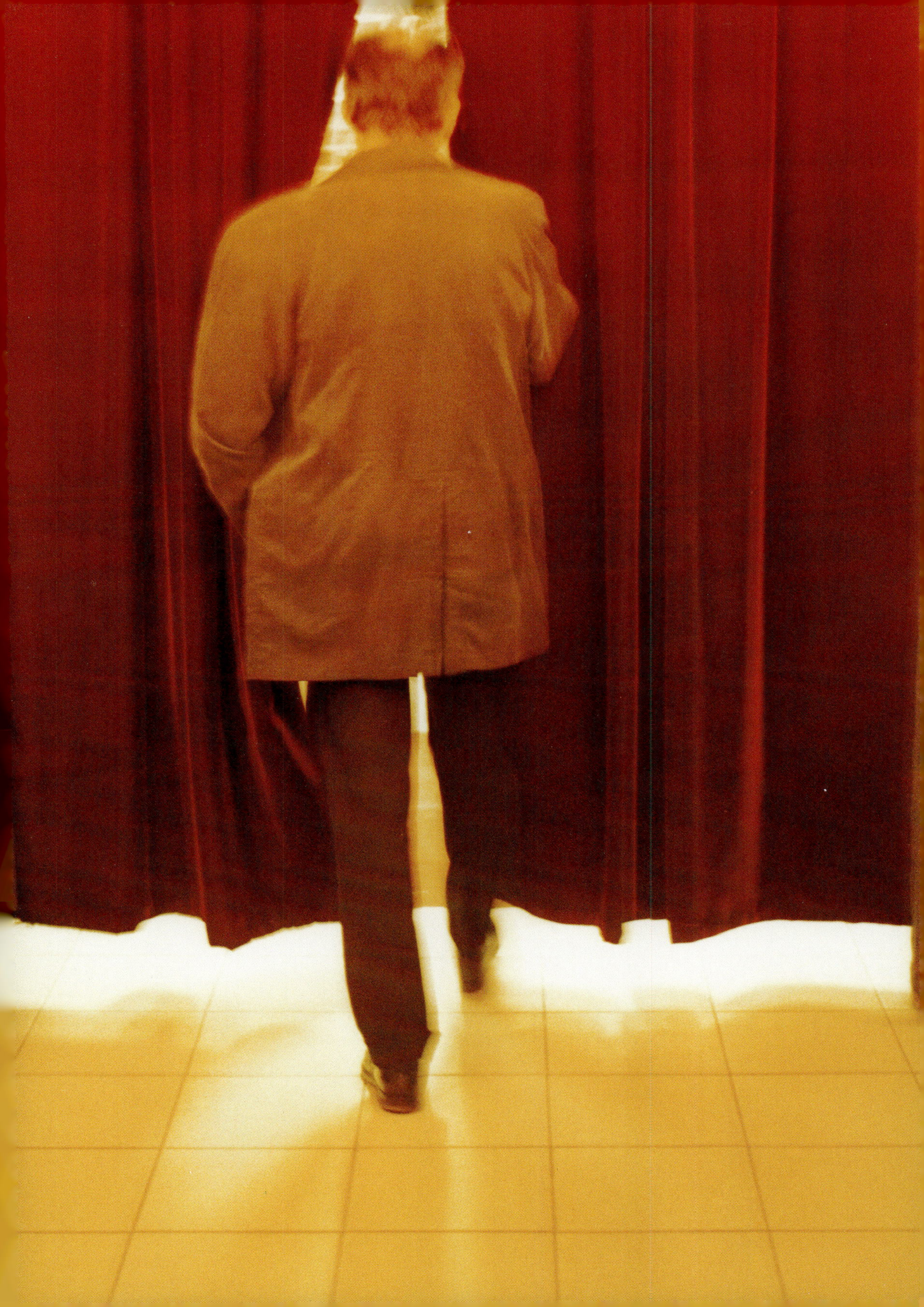

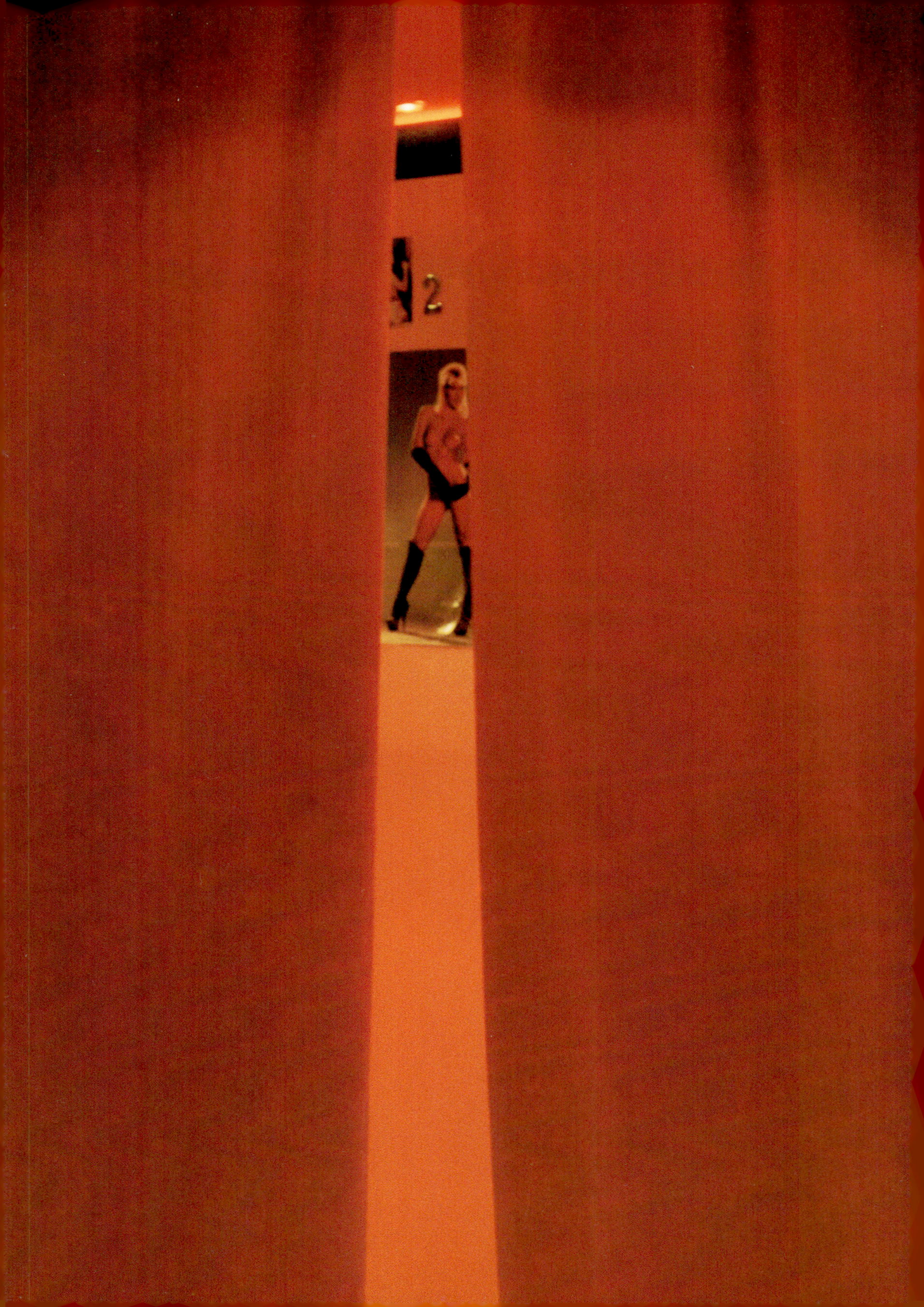
2

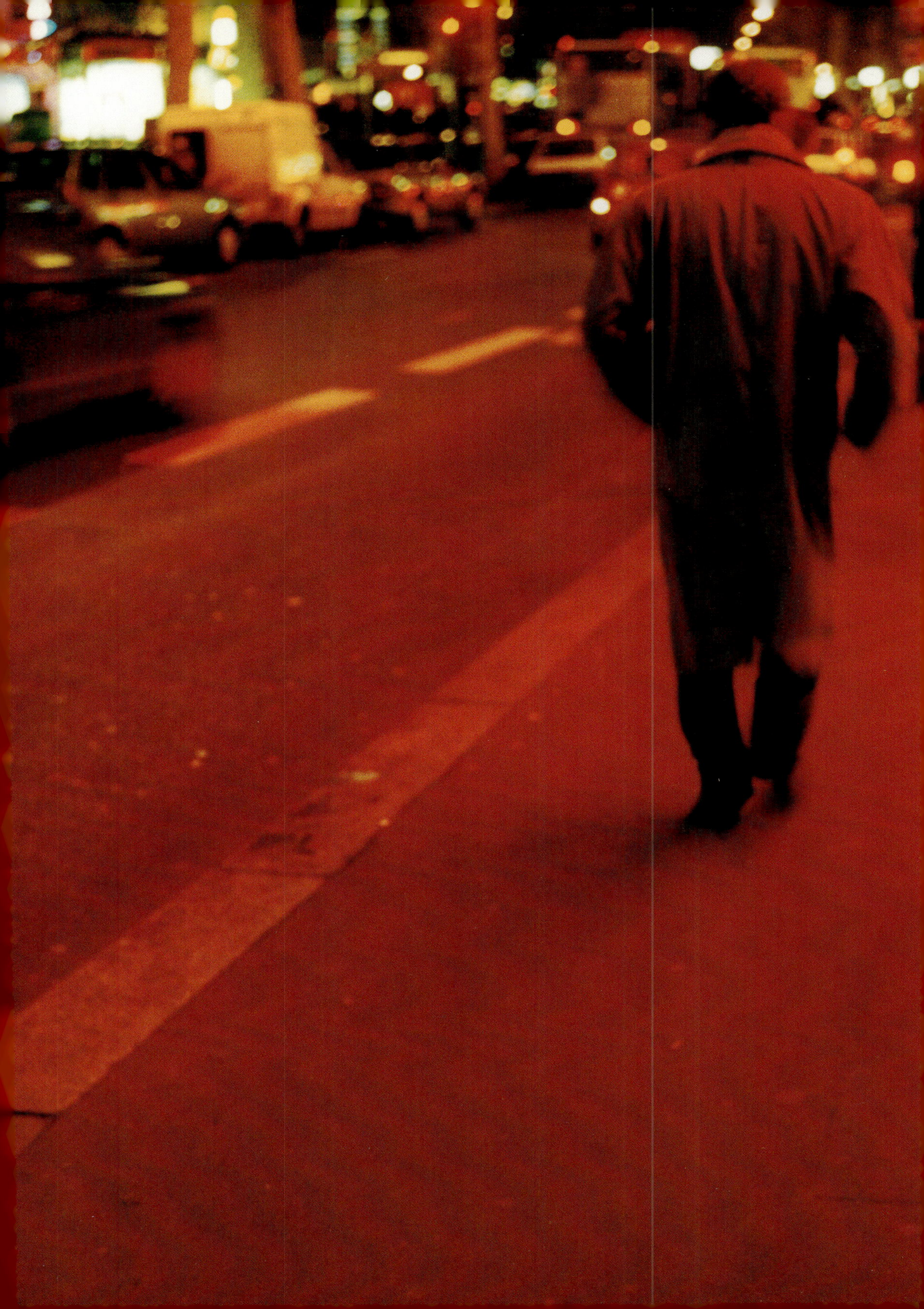

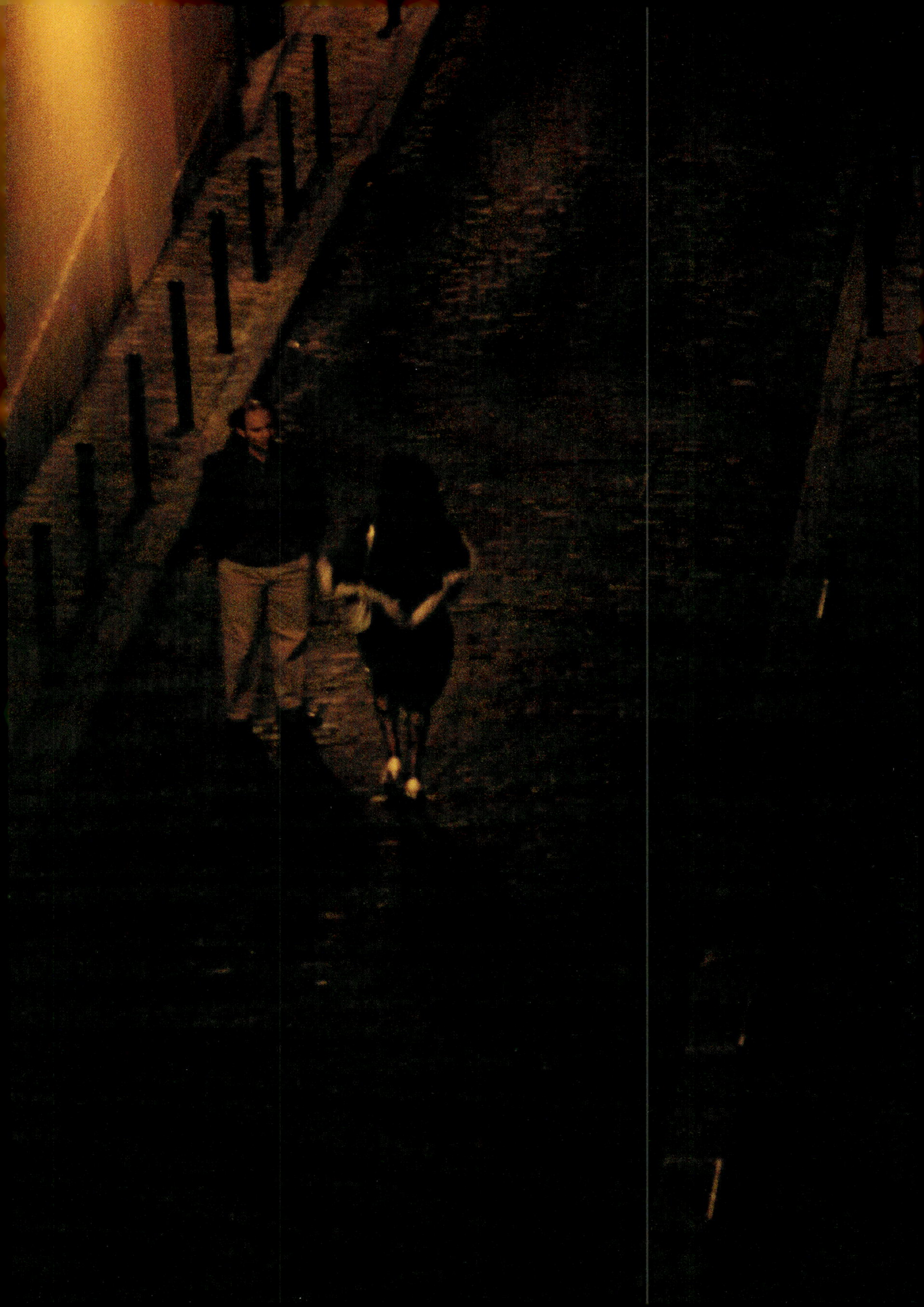

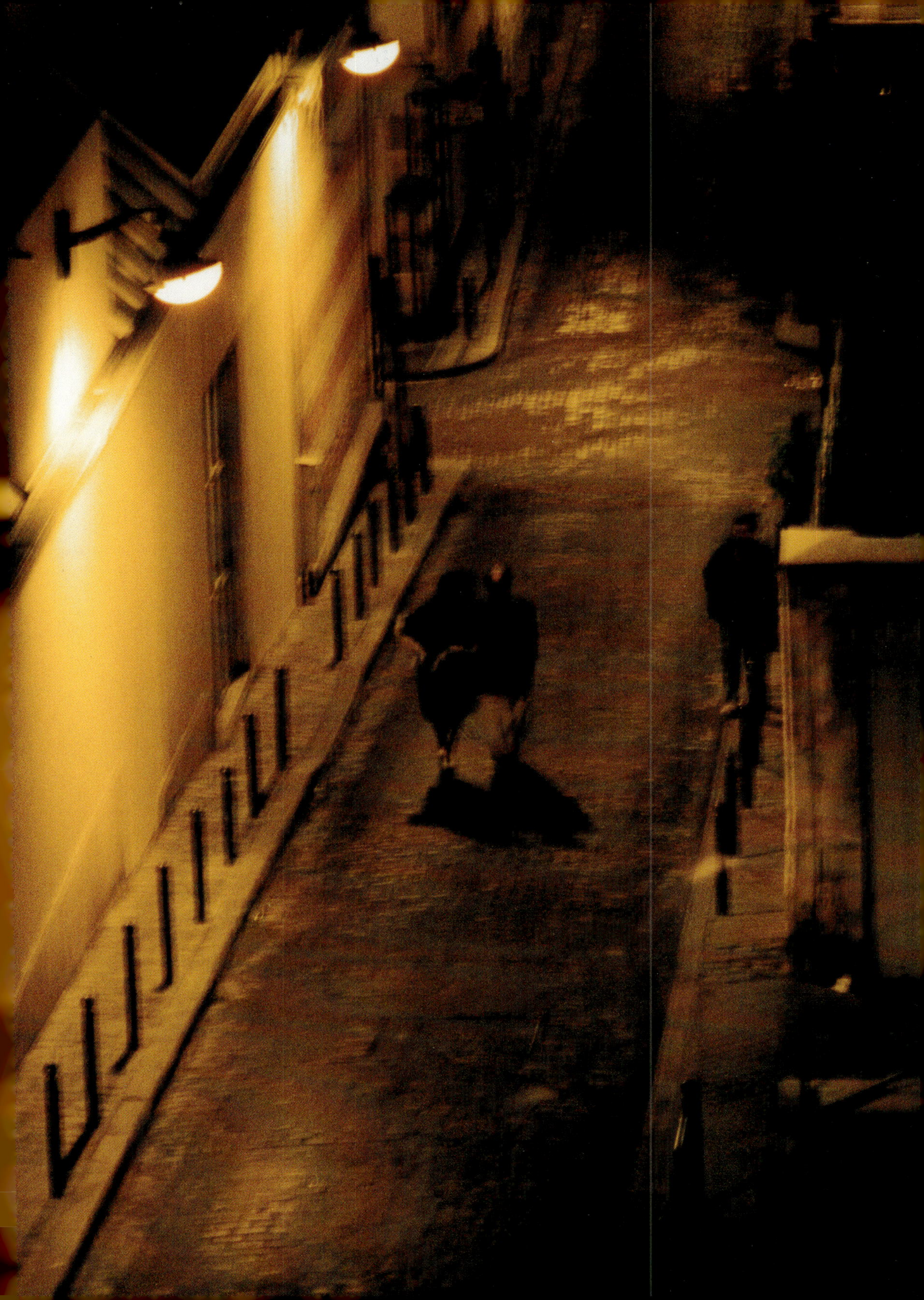

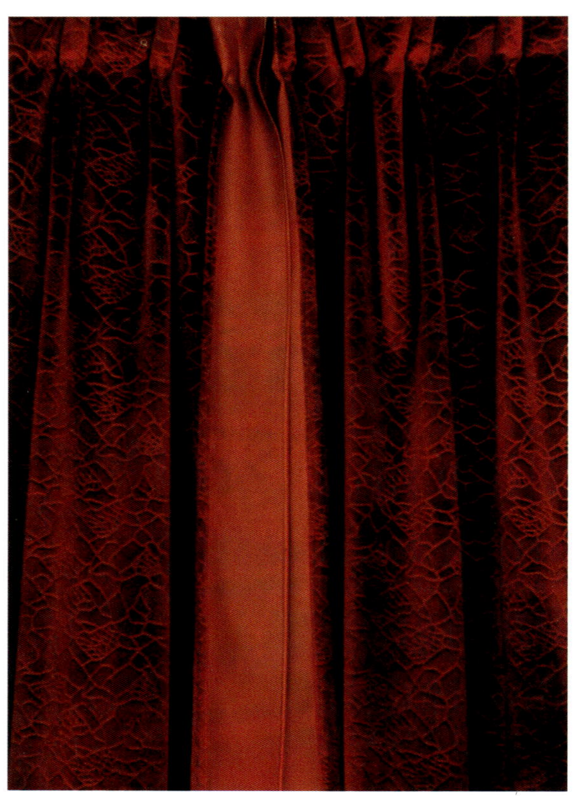